The Wedding Collection

THE
WEDDING
COLLECTION

Morris H. Chapman
Compiler

BROADMAN PRESS
NASHVILLE, TENNESSEE

© Copyright 1991 • Broadman Press
All rights reserved
4220-04

ISBN: 0-8054-2004-5
Dewey Decimal Classification: 252.1
Subject Heading: WEDDINGS
Library of Congress Catalog Number: 91-18637
Printed in the United States of America

Unless otherwise indicated, all Scripture references are from the *King James Version* of the Bible.

Scripture quotations marked (NIV) are from HOLY BIBLE *New International Version*, copyright © 1978, New York Bible Society. Used by permission.

Scripture quotations marked (TLB) are from *The Living Bible*. Copyright © Tyndale House Publishers, Wheaton, Illinois, 1971. Used by permission.

The Scripture quotation marked (NKJV) is from the *New King James Version*. Copyright © 1979, 1980, 1982, Thomas Nelson, Inc., Publishers.

Scripture quotations marked (NASB) are from the *New American Standard Bible*, © The Lockman Foundation, 1960, 1962, 1963, 1975, 1977. Used by permission.

Library of Congress Cataloging-in-Publication Data

Chapman, Morris.
   The wedding collection / Morris H. Chapman.
      p. c.m.
   ISBN 0-8054-2004-5 : $11.95
   1. Wedding service. 2. Baptists—Liturgy—Texts. I. Title.
BX6337.C48   1991
265'.5—dc20   91-18637
                                                                              CIP

To
Jodi Francis Chapman
My beautiful bride
My loving wife
My best friend

Preface

The Wedding Collection easily could have been entitled *A Celebration of Love!* Very few experiences in life are quite so momentous, so beautiful, so hopeful. Laughter reverberates through the hectic hours of preparation.

As the time approaches, nerves tighten and emotions run high. The pulse quickens, the heart pounds, the eyes glisten. Finally, the hour arrives. The bride envisions the ceremony to be a long and lasting tribute to the couple's love for each other, but most grooms are given to asking, "How long will the ceremony last?" No matter how long or short the ceremony, the wedding ever so quickly merges into marriage.

God intended for both the wedding and the marriage to be a celebration of love. For the wedding to be a genuine celebration, both the bride and the groom must come to the altar, already having invited Jesus Christ into their hearts. For the marriage to be a lifelong celebration, the couple must remember through the years to place the other before self and Christ above all.

To love without expecting anything in return is unconditional love and a necessary ingredient to a happy marriage.

These ceremonies have been compiled with the prayer that the bride and groom will find them helpful in the preparation of a wedding ceremony which will become an expression of their personal thoughts. Some will find within these pages a ceremony which will be "perfect" for them. Others may choose to put together an "original," combining parts of several ceremonies with their own ideas.

I pray also that these ceremonies will be a timely resource for my fellow pastors and to all ministers who are called upon to conduct weddings. The one who is officiating may read directly from this manual. Or, he may wish to copy the ceremony onto other sheets of paper. Perhaps he will prefer to incorporate phrases and/or paragraphs from these ceremonies in creating his own unique wedding ceremony.

However the book is utilized, may God bless those who have the privilege of offering wise words of godly counsel to couples preparing to be married. With the help of my minister friends across the country, I have prayerfully accumulated these wedding ceremonies over a period of time. To each of these, my beloved brothers in Christ, I am most grateful. I pray these ceremonies will be a blessing to all who read them.

I give thanks to Suzy Lee for proofreading the manuscript. I am especially thankful to my secretary, Barbara Schaefer, for assisting me in preparing the manuscript for *The Wedding Collection* and for her significant role in my ministry as an executive assistant.

Most of all, I give praise and thanksgiving to our dear Lord Jesus Christ who first loved us and sanctified the lifetime covenant of love called marriage.

—MORRIS H. CHAPMAN
The Pastor's Study
First Baptist Church
Wichita Falls, Texas

Contents

The Ten Commandments of Marriage

I. When God gave us the Ten Commandments (Ex. 20:11-17) He said, "I am the Lord thy God . . . thou shalt have no other gods before me" (20:3). Surely the Lord would have us to honor that in marriage. No other human being should come before your mate—no one, neither father nor mother, son nor daughter, brother nor sister, friend nor acquaintance. So, the First Commandment of Marriage is: "Thou shalt have no other human being before your husband or your wife."

II. God's Word teaches: "Thou shalt not make unto thee any graven image" (20:4). In like fashion you should put no thing between each other. No house should ever come before your spouse. A housewife does not marry a house; she marries a man. Foolish is the woman who puts her house above her "house-band." Therefore, the Second Commandment of Marriage is, "Thou shalt put no thing before your husband or your wife," whether car, pleasure, money, or fame—nothing."

III. The Third Commandment declares, "Thou shalt not take the name of the Lord thy God in vain" (20:7). Then, the Third Commandment of Marriage is: "Thou shalt not belittle, criticize or faultfind, but rather encourage your spouse in all ways." Since God's Word teaches us to make no idols, it follows that we are to honor each other's name. Honor each other and seek to put each other first above any other person on earth, remembering always that in all things Christ must have preeminence (see Col. 1:18). The Scriptures declare with irresistible logic that those who judge will be judged and will bring back upon their heads the bitterness they project. Do not belittle each other's name, person, sexuality, desires, or dreams.

IV. The Bible further commands, "Remember the sabbath day, to keep it holy" (20:8). We are to remember God's day. Likewise I would urge you to remember her/his day. The Fourth Commandment of Marriage is, "Thou shalt remember her/his day, to keep it special." Set time aside religiously that the two of you may not grow apart but even closer. Your spouse and your children are worthy of your time and your undivided attention.

V. God's Word teaches, "Honor thy father and thy mother: that thy days may be long upon the land which the Lord thy God giveth thee" (20:12). As the two of you become one, you marry into another family. The Fifth Commandment of Marriage is: "Thou shalt give honor not only to your father and mother, but to those who become your father-in-law and mother-in-law." Wise is the husband or wife who does not take it upon himself or herself to find fault with those who are related to their spouse.

VI. The Sixth Commandment emphatically states, "Thou shalt not kill" (20:13). The Sixth Commandment of Marriage is, "Thou shalt not destroy the spirit within your spouse."

_____ (Groom), do not destroy your bride's dreams and her hopes for the future which she now places in your hands. Most of man's earthly happiness depends upon his wife. Most assuredly God will bless a man in this life, yet John Wesley discovered that, regardless of a noble cause, a woman can make a man most miserable. _____ (Bride), covenant that you will not be such a person. Both of you must honor and build up the personhood of the other.

VII. God commanded, "Thou shalt not commit adultery" (20:14). The Seventh Commandment of Marriage is: "Thou shalt give your passions only to each other, not to another." You should not give away your passions to another in word, in thought, or in deed. This person beside whom you stand on this wedding day is to be your lover as well as your helpmate and your friend.

VIII. Another commandment of our Lord is: "Thou shalt not steal" (20:15). _____ (Groom), steal not from your wife that which it is her privilege to give. _____ (Bride), receive what he gives to you with gratitude. The spirit of gratitude can greatly bless a home. If your minds are filled with thoughts of gratitude, and if you look on that which you do have and not that which you do not have, you will be blessed.

IX. The Bible teaches, "Thou shalt not bear false witness against thy neighbor" (20:16). The Ninth Commandment of Marriage is: "Thou shalt not bear false witness to each other." Be honest with each other. Dishonesty and an unwillingness to talk through differences build a silent wall which is not easily dismantled. The real self, then, refuses to be disclosed, and a couple may gradually begin to drift apart.

X. The final commandment says: "Thou shalt not covet" (20:17). The Tenth Commandment of Marriage is, "Thou shalt not seek greener pastures, whether they be those things physical or material." Do not engage in selfish fantasies. Be content with the one whom God has given to you, and God will bless your lives together.

I believe, as you seek to follow Jesus Christ and join hands with Him and with each other, your home will be sanctified, and His love will fill not only your hearts but also your home. May that home be a place of blessing where those who come within its portals shall find the love of Christ reigning supreme.

D. James Kennedy, Pastor
Coral Ridge Presbyterian Church
Fort Lauderdale, Florida

Ceremony 1

This is the actual ceremony of Morris and Jodi Chapman's daughter, Stephanie, to Anthony Scott Evans, November 3, 1990.

Processional

Testimony (Jonathan Beasley)

Two and one-half years ago I had the privilege of being in a small church with my friend Scott. I have the special bond of having been there when he accepted the Lord as his personal Savior. A little while later I received a call from Dr. Chapman inquiring about a young man named Scott for his daughter Stephanie! I had only good things to say because of what Christ had done in his heart. When I called Stephanie to talk with her about Scott I was warmed by the thoughts which she shared. She said that both she and Scott were focusing their relationship on the person of Jesus Christ. As a friend, I want to commend both of you. You have been a wonderful example to me, and I love you both.

Who gives this woman to be married to this man?

Response (father of the bride): Her mother and I.

Welcome (Father of the Bride)

A wedding is a celebration of love. Scott and Stephanie are most grateful for your presence on this day when they pledge their lifelong love to each other. Your very presence symbolizes your love for them. The love felt in this place flows from the heart of God. The greatest love story ever told is found in these simple words, "For God so loved the world" (John 3:16). The deepest love known to man is the love of God. We love because He first loved us.

Biblical Foundation of Marriage

The Bible says, "Therefore as the church is subject unto Christ, so let the wives be to their own husbands in every thing. Husbands, love your wives, even as Christ also loved the church [His bride] and gave himself for it" (Eph. 5:24-25). We are assembled in this place where we worship God and where we preach Jesus Christ and Him crucified (see 1 Cor. 2:2).

These two persons would have chosen no other place to declare the love of their hearts for each other, for they both believe Jesus to be the

Son of God and their Savior. Thus, Scott and Stephanie are already united in Christ as believers. They are bound together in love for Christ and His church. Now that bond takes on a new and beautiful dimension through the covenant of marriage. They believe their love for each other was initiated from above and is a gift from God. Because of their deep conviction that God has drawn them together for His divine purposes, we come with abundant joy to thank Him for what He has done in their lives and to entrust their future to Him.

Scott and *Stephanie*, if indeed your love runs as deeply as you have heretofore expressed, please join right hands.

In all of life, rare is the moment that is filled with more hope, more joy, and more expectancy than this sacred moment. By God's design this moment is never to be repeated, but rather always to be cherished. The vows you are about to make will be locked in your memories as a reminder that you have pledged to love for a lifetime the one who stands willingly and expectantly beside you. Through the years, your remembrance of this moment is intended to strengthen your marriage and to cause you to give thanks to God for having each other.

Scott, will you have this woman to be your wedded wife, to live together after God's ordinance, in the holy estate of matrimony? Will you love her, honor and keep her, in sickness and in health; and forsaking all others keep yourself only for her, so long as you both shall live?

Response: I will.

Stephanie, will you have this man to be your wedded husband, to live together after God's ordinance, in the holy estate of matrimony? Will you serve him, love, honor, and keep him in sickness and in health; and forsaking all others keep yourself only for him, so long as you both shall live?

Response: I will.

Scott and *Stephanie,* God loves you both. He has saved you for the life to come and He has given you each other for as long as you both shall live in this life. I know your families love you. Our hearts will be filled with parental pride as you continue to find and fulfill God's plan for your lives. Our prayers will find their way to the throne of grace and God will grant us assurance of His provision and protection for you. From the moment we learned you were to be born, you have been in our prayers. Now we rejoice with you in yet another answer to our prayers and yours.

You are preparing to walk in the way which has been God's design from the beginning of time. God's Word declares, "Therefore shall a man leave his father and his mother, and shall cleave unto his wife: and they shall be one flesh" (Gen. 2:24).

Scott, leaving your parents is for the purpose of leading your wife. To cleave to your wife is to cling to her for life. The Bible says, "Let thy fountain be blessed: and rejoice with the wife of thy youth" (Prov. 6:18). Again the Bible says, "Husbands . . . in the same way be considerate as you live with your wives, and treat them with respect as the weaker partner and as heirs with you in the gracious gift of life, so that nothing will hinder your prayers" (1 Pet. 3:7, NIV).

Scott, as you accept the love of this young woman, my daughter, I ask you to remember to show love and compassion and to care for her in the many small ways which touch a woman's heart. Although you are charged by God Himself to be the head of your home, remember to listen to your wife and to value her opinions. These opinions will come from one whose very heart beats for your best and whose desire is to please you and encourage you. Praise her in your home and praise her in the company of others. Before you can lead your wife and your children in knowing Christ better and loving Him more, you must first "set your affection on things above, not on things on the earth" (Col. 3:2).

God's Word also says, "Wives . . . your beauty . . . should be that of your inner self, the unfading beauty of a gentle and quiet spirit, which is of great worth in God's sight. For this is the way the holy women of the past who put their hope in God used to make themselves beautiful. They were submissive to their own husbands" (1 Pet. 3:4-5, NIV).

Stephanie, as you receive the love of this young man, my son-in-law, I ask you to remember to love him with the tenderness of a woman's touch, to speak softly, yet honestly and to reassure him of your undying devotion. Let him see the beauty which comes from deep within the heart of a woman who loves Jesus.

Vows

I, *Scott*, take thee, *Stephanie*, to my wedded wife, to have and to hold, from this day forward, for better for worse, for richer for poorer, in sickness and in health, to love and to cherish, till death do us part, according to God's holy ordinance, and thereto I pledge thee my love.

One of the most beautiful pictures of love and devotion from one heart to another is expressed by the words of Ruth when she said, "Entreat me not to leave thee, or to return from following after thee: for whither thou goest, I will go; and where thou lodgest, I will lodge: thy people shall be my people, and thy God my God" (Ruth 1:16).

I, _Stephanie_, take thee, _Scott_, to my wedded husband, to have and to hold, from this day forward, for better for worse, for richer for poorer, in sickness and in health, to love and to cherish, till death do us part, according to God's holy ordinance, and thereto I pledge thee my love.

"Love is patient, love is kind. It does not envy, it does not boast, it is not proud. It is not rude, it is not self-seeking, it is not easily angered, it keeps no record of wrongs. Love does not delight in evil but rejoices with the truth. It always protects, always trusts, always hopes, always perseveres. Love never fails" (1 Cor. 13:4-8_a_, NIV).

Exchange of Rings

The wedding ring is devoted to the beautiful purpose of symbolizing your covenant to love each other and to live together for as long as you both shall live. The ring is an unending circle which symbolizes a love between you that shall never cease. The ring's untarnished gold represents the lasting quality of your love, a love that shall never grow old.

Scott

With this ring, I thee wed, and with all my worldly goods, I thee endow; in the name of the

Father, and of the Son, and of the Holy Spirit.
Amen.

   Stephanie

I give this ring to my beloved, as a token of
my love, now and forever; in the name of the
Father, and of the Son, and of the Holy Spirit.
Amen.

Prayer Song

(A prayer song is sung while the couple
kneels at the kneeling bench.)

Pastoral Prayer

(Couple continues to kneel.)

Pronouncement

(The couple stands, facing each other, and the
groom takes both hands of the bride into his
hands. A song of commitment is sung while
they look into each other's eyes.)

Please forgive me for taking a moment of personal privilege. Every bride is very, very beautiful, but never have I seen one with quite the
glow of this bride! Thank you for rejoicing with
us in this wedding. These are two very fine
young people whom God has drawn together.
Scott, I would ask you only to love my daughter
as much as I have loved her and her mother.

Stephanie, I would ask you only to love *Scott* as much as your mother has loved your father.

Scott and *Stephanie,* on the basis of your covenant of love and by the authority given me as a minister of the gospel of the living Christ, and in accordance with the laws of the State of Texas, I pronounce you husband and wife, in the name of the Father, and of the Son, and of the Holy Spirit. "What therefore God hath joined together, let not man put asunder" (Mark 10:9).

You may kiss your bride. (Couple turns to face the guests.) I introduce you to Mr. and Mrs. Anthony Scott Evans.

Recessional

Morris H. Chapman (Father of the Bride)
Pastor, First Baptist Church
Wichita Falls, Texas

Ceremony 2

Processional

Introduction

When two hearts are bound together in the bonds of Christian matrimony, it is a blessed and sacred moment. We recognize that marriage is an important part of God's plan for mankind. God Himself long ago ordained and instituted marriage, and it was He who performed the first wedding ceremony in the garden of Eden.

When our Lord Jesus Christ came into this world He chose a wedding at Cana in Galilee to perform His first mighty miracle. In order to achieve success in this, the highest of all human commitments, we must look to God's Word for direction. The Bible says that you are to submit yourselves one to another in the fear of God. Wives, you are to submit yourselves unto your own husbands, as unto the Lord, for the husband is the head of the wife, even as Christ is the head of the church, and He is the Savior of the body.

Husbands, love your wives even as Christ also loved the church and gave Himself for it. A man shall leave his father and mother and shall be joined unto his wife and they two shall be one flesh.

The beautiful love you share with each other is described in 1 Corinthians 13. There the Bible says, "Love is very patient and kind, never jealous or envious, never boastful or proud, never haughty or selfish or rude. Love does not demand its own way. It is not irritable or touchy. It does not hold grudges and will hardly even notice when others do wrong. It is never glad about injustice, but rejoices whenever truth wins out. If you love someone you will be loyal to him no matter what the cost. You will always believe in him, always expect the best of him, and always stand your ground in defending him. All the special gifts and powers from God will someday come to an end, but love goes on forever. Someday prophecy, and speaking in unknown languages, and special knowledge—these gifts will disappear. There are three things that remain—faith, hope, and love—and the greatest of these is love" (1 Cor. 13:4-8,13, TLB).

Vows

So if you, _____ (groom) and _____
(bride) have come signifying your desire to be
formally united in the bonds of Christian matrimony, will you now join both hands, and remember the closer you keep Christ in the center
of your life, the greater your love will be for the
other?

_____ (groom) in taking _____
(bride) to be your lawful and wedded wife, before God and these witnesses present, you
must promise to love her, to honor and cherish
her, and leaving all others, to cleave only to her
and be to her in all things the true and faithful
husband so long as you both shall live. Do you
so promise?

Response: I do.

_____ (bride) in taking _____
(groom) to be your lawful and wedded husband, before God and these witnesses present,
you must promise to love him, to honor and
cherish him and leaving all others, to cleave
only to him and be to him in all things the true
and faithful wife so long as you both shall live.
Do you so promise?

Response: I do.

Then, you are each given to the other. In
times of happiness and in times of sorrow; in

times of plenty and in times of poverty; in times of sickness and in times of well being; to love and enjoy till death shall separate you.

Exchange of Rings

May I have the rings please?

From time immemorial the ring has been used to seal this most important of all human commitments. The ring is a beautiful symbol of your love, in that it is an unending circle symbolizing the eternity of your love, and the purity of gold in the ring symbolizes the purity of your love in God's eyes in the marriage relationship.

_____ (groom), will you take this ring which is a beautiful symbol and meaningful token of your love for _____ (bride) and place it on the ring finger of her left hand and while holding it in place repeat these words to her? "With this ring I thee wed, with loyal love I thee endow, and all my worldly goods with thee I share, in the name of the Father, the Son and the Holy Spirit. Amen."

_____ (bride), this ring is a beautiful symbol and meaningful token of your love for _____ (groom). Will you now place it on the ring finger of his left hand and while holding it in place repeat these words to him? "With this ring I thee wed, with loyal love I thee endow, and all my worldly goods with thee I share, in the Name of the Father, the Son, and the Holy Spirit. Amen."

Prayer

Pronouncement

Now, having pledged your faith in each other and love for each other, and having sealed that pledge through the exchange of these rings, and by your solemn vows to each other before God, I, acting in the authority vested in me as a minister of the gospel, am looking to God for His divine approval upon your life, and pronounce you husband and wife. "What therefore God hath joined together, let not man put asunder" (Mark 10:9).

Recessional

> Stan Coffey, Pastor
> San Jacinto Baptist Church
> Amarillo, Texas

Ceremony 3

Processional

Introduction

Dearly beloved, we are gathered together here in the sight of God and these witnesses, to join together this man and this woman in the holy estate of matrimony. The Bible teaches that marriage was created by God. He made an helpmate for Adam and called her woman, for she was taken from the man. In the Old Testament, Moses, the lawgiver, gave divine sanction to marriage as a legal institution. In the New Testament, the Book of Hebrews says that marriage is honorable among all. Therefore, because God has put His blessing upon this union, and this is a service of Christian worship celebrating the work of God, let us pause to ask for God's blessing and presence in this service.

Prayer

The Bible declares that marriage is a type of the mystical union that exists between Christ and the church. It is an earthly portrayal of a heavenly reality. Hear the words of the apostle Paul from the Book of Ephesians.

"And do not be drunk with wine in which is dissipation, but be filled with the Spirit, speaking to one another in psalms and hymns and spiritual songs, singing and making melody in your heart to the Lord, giving thanks always for all things to God the Father in the name of our Lord Jesus Christ, submitting to one another in the fear of God. Wives, submit to your own husbands as to the Lord, for the husband is the head of the wife, as also Christ is head of the church, and He is the Savior of the body. Therefore, just as the church is subject unto Christ, so let the wives be to their own husbands in everything. Husbands, love your wives, just as Christ also loved the church and gave Himself for it, that He might sanctify and cleanse it with the washing of water by the Word, that He might present it to Himself a glorious church, not having spot or wrinkle, or any such thing, but that it should be holy and without blemish. So husbands ought to love their own wives as their own bodies. He who loves his wife loves himself, for no one ever hated his own flesh but nourishes and cherishes it just as the Lord does the church, for we are members of His body, of His flesh, and of His bones. For this reason a man shall leave his father and mother and be joined to his wife and the two shall become one flesh (Eph. 5:18-31).

Parents's Charge

(An option which is inserted periodically is a charge to the parents. This is becoming more popular and can be used in the following manner.)

Will the parents please stand for the charge to the parents? Will you respond at the conclusion of the charge?

Response: We do.

With gratitude for your love, support, and nurture through the years, this couple comes today to form a new family under God's blessing. Do you grant to them the freedom to form a new family and seek God's blessing? Do you grant them the freedom to form a new family and seek God's will? Do you pledge to them your continuing love and support? Do you promise to be quick to listen and slow to speak, and do you covenant to pray for them and the ministry God plans for them in the future?

Response: We do. (Parents may now be seated.)

(A brief extemporaneous exposition of the main points of the Scripture previously read is then given while the wedding party is all gathered at the front, usually at the lower level of the sanctuary, before the bride, groom, pastor, best man, and maid of honor go to the upper level. The following is a sample of the kind of brief miniexposition that is given.)

Paul gives us guidance on this most intimate of relationships in this passage. First, he states that we should not depend upon drugs, liquor, money, or any externals for joy and happiness in life, but rather let our lives and our marriage be filled with the Holy Spirit. That means: let the Spirit of God have control of our lives and marriages. Let Him fill up this relationship. Make room for Christ in the home you are establishing.

Then in the next verse the apostle encourages Christians to communicate to one another about the deepest spiritual things of life with psalms, hymns, and spiritual songs. Two happy people with a song in their hearts because Christ is in control of their lives make good material for a godly marriage. Learn to communicate with each other beyond the superficial. Talk about the things God is doing in each of your lives, and share the things you are thinking, the dreams you are dreaming, the problems you are facing, the burdens you are bearing.

In the next verse the apostle encourages us to

maintain an attitude of thanks. If God the Father is a sovereign God, there is not anything that happens to your marriage that you cannot give thanks for it, knowing He is capable of bringing good into your lives out of it. After you are married you will discover things about each other you did not know. You will want to focus on the positive things. Give thanks for your marriage in spite of the fact that there are surprises and begin to trust God for victory over the surprises.

Next, the apostle Paul encourages married couples to submit themselves to each other in the fear of God. Before the Scripture admonishes women to be subject to their husbands, the Bible lays down something very fundamental to the Christian faith. We should be in *mutual submission* to each other in the fear, or the reverence, of God; that is, out of respect for God. It is true in a local church that members have obligations and responsibilities to one another. So it is in a Christian marriage. We are to be willing to set aside our needs, our wants, and our interests for the good of the other. A Christian husband will never have a problem leading his family if he has convinced his family that he is willing to set aside his best interests for their best interests in order to help them achieve their potential. That is what each of you must do for the other, and you will demonstrate servant-hood in marriage and eliminate competition.

Then the Scripture says, "Wives, submit to your own husbands." This is the picture of the church's attitude toward Christ who is her Head. A body of believers called a church joy-fully submits to the leadership of its head, Christ, because it trusts Him, and it knows He will always do it well. The Scripture does not here command a woman to love her husband, because that is not her danger. The danger, rather, for a woman is that if her husband doesn't provide the leadership she desires, she will take over the headship, and soon her hus-band may feel emasculated. Let him be the leader. Encourage him to take responsibility. Many a marriage has broken up because a man felt he was not a man in his own home, and, Sir, if you will love your wife and are submissive to her needs, it is her nature to love you, and that is why God does not have to command her to love you in this passage.

In the next verse husbands are admonished to love their wives as Christ loved the church. He loved the church before the church loved Him, and He loved it without any conditions. It was sacrificial love, with no idea of reward. In fact, He loved the church enough to die for it, and, Sir, I charge you this day in the fashion of

Christ, take the initiative to love her. There is not a marriage problem that any couple faces that cannot be helped by a man learning how to more fully and adequately love his wife in the pattern of Christ and with the power of the Holy Spirit.

She feels more secure and protected when she knows you love her. The husband's danger is that he will become so involved in his work or his hobbies that he will take his wife for granted. The Scripture declares that you must never take her for granted. That is one thing a woman cannot long tolerate. You should love her as you love yourself; nourishing, providing, cherishing, protecting her, granting her not only security and protection from the world, but creating a climate for growth in which your wife can achieve her highest potential for the glory of God.

There are other instructions in the Scriptures. A man is to provide for his own and especially for those of his own house. If he does not, then he has denied the faith and is "worse than an infidel." The Bible teaches that a man has not power over his own body, but the woman: and likewise also the woman has not power over her own body, but the man. Proverbs 31 states that a godly woman will care for the ways of her husband and her household, and if she does, and if the Lord chooses to grant her children, both the children and her husband will rise up to call her blessed.

May the Lord bless you as from this day forward you seek to carry out these scriptural ideals of your marriage. We shall pray for you that the Lord will enable you to do the things we have read today.

In light of the serious approach the Scriptures take toward marriage, it should be entered into with sobriety and reverence. If any man can show just cause why this couple should not be joined together, let him speak now or else, hereafter and forever, hold his peace.

Who gives this woman to be married to this man?

Response: Her mother and I.

Vows

_____ (groom), do you take this woman to be your lawfully wedded wife, to live together after God's ordinance in the holy estate of matrimony? Do you promise from this day forward to provide for her spiritual leadership? Do you promise to perform unto her all the obligations and responsibilities of a Christian husband? Do you pledge yourself to love her, comfort her, honor and keep her, in sickness and in health, and forsaking all others, keep yourself only for her so long as you both shall live?

Response: I do.

_____ (bride), do you take this man to your lawfully wedded husband, to live together after God's ordinance in the holy estate of matrimony? Do you promise from this day forward to follow him as your spiritual leader? Do you promise to perform unto him all the obligations and responsibilities of a Christian wife? Do you pledge to love him, comfort him, honor and keep him, in sickness and in health, and forsaking all others, keep yourself only for him so long as you both shall live?

Response: I do.

(The immediate wedding party, consisting of pastor, bride and groom, best man, and maid of honor will now proceed to the upper level, and if so desired, congregate around the kneeling bench which is used later in the ceremony.)

In the great love chapter of 1 Corinthians 13, we read the following:

Though I speak with the tongues of men and of angels, and have not love, I am become as sounding brass or a clanging cymbal. And though I have the gift of prophecy, and understand all mysteries and all knowledge, and though I have all faith so that I could remove mountains, but have not love, I am nothing. And though I bestow all my goods to feed the poor, and though I give my body to be burned, but have not love, it profits me nothing. Love suffers long and is kind. Love does not envy. Love does not parade itself, is not puffed up, does not behave rudely, does not seek his own, is not provoked, thinks no evil, does not rejoice in iniquity, but rejoices in the truth. Love bears all things, believes all things, hopes all things, endures all things. Love never fails (1 Cor. 13:1-8*a*, NKJV).

Rings

What symbols do you bring to this altar of your love for each other? (The best man and maid of honor will hand the rings to the pastor.) Please note that these rings are perfect circles having no beginning or ending. As such they represent the eternal nature of God who also has no beginning or ending. If God is eternal and God is love, then love is eternal. If love is eternal, then love is unconditional. God loves each of us without any conditions. There is no way we can make God quit loving us since it is

His nature to love. His love is not based upon our performance but upon His nature.

The love you have for each other also comes from God, and He wants you to practice love toward each other in the same way He loves you. To God, love is obedient action. He wants you to love each other unconditionally without any idea of reward. As you wear these rings, let them serve as reminders to you in the hard moments of your love and life that love is of God and is nourished and sustained for each other as you both live close to Him. But these rings also are made of valuable metal. They represent something of great value in your life. It is the high priority God wants you to give to this relationship with each other. After your relationship to God, nothing else in life can be as important as the nurture and the maintenance of this godly relationship of marriage. There is no job, there is no hobby, there is no ambition that is more important than the success of a godly marriage. So as you exchange these rings, I charge you to place a high priority upon the maintenance of this godly married relationship you are establishing this day. (The pastor then hands the rings to the bride and groom.)

Please turn and face each other for the ring exchange. What token do you bring, _____

(groom), of your love and affection for
_____ (bride)?

The man shall answer: "This ring." Please
place it upon her finger, hold it there, and repeat after me: "With this ring I thee wed—in the
name of the Father, and of the Son, and of the
Holy Spirit. Amen."

What token do you bring, _____ (bride),
of your love and affection for _____
(groom)? The woman shall answer: "This ring."
Please place it on his finger, hold it there, and
repeat after me: "With this ring I thee wed, in
the name of the Father, and of the Son, and of
the Holy Spirit. Amen."

While you are facing each other, please join
hands and repeat after me your personal vows.
I, _____ (groom), take thee, _____
(bride), to be my wedded wife, to have and to
hold, from this day forward, for better, for
worse, for richer, for poorer, in sickness and in
health, to love and to cherish until death do us
part."

"I, _____ (bride), take thee, _____
(groom), to be my wedded husband, to have
and to hold, from this day forward, for better,
for worse, for richer, for poorer, in sickness and
in health, to love and to cherish, until death do
us part."

(The unity candle ceremony is optional here.)

Unity Candle

The ancient candle ceremony symbolizes the one-flesh principle in Christian marriage. The two become one and treat each other as if they were a part of their own flesh.

(The couple moves to the unity candle and while the pastor recites the Ruth passage or an appropriate song is sung, they light the center candle together.)

The love that comes out of this sort of unity is best described by Ruth's words to Naomi in the Old Testament: "Intreat me not to leave thee, or to return from following after thee: for whither thou goest, I will go; and where thou lodgest, I will lodge: thy people shall be my people, and thy God my God. Where thou diest will I die, and there will I be buried: the Lord do so to me, and more also if aught but death part thee and me" (Ruth 1:16-17).

In Christ the two become one.

Prayer

(The couple will kneel at the kneeling bench if a bench is used. Otherwise they will stand for the prayer. The prayer is always extemporaneous. An option is that, at the conclusion of the prayer while the couple is kneeling, the Lord's Prayer may be sung.)

Pronouncement

Will you please stand? By the authority vested in me as a minister of the gospel of Jesus Christ, in accordance with the vows you have taken each to the other, and by virtue of the laws of the state of _____, I joyfully pronounce you husband and wife, and what God has joined together, let no man ever put asunder.

"The Lord bless you and keep you. The Lord make his face to shine upon you and be gracious to you. The Lord lift up his countenance upon you and give you peace" (Num. 6:24-26, NKJV).

You may kiss the bride.

As the couple turns and joins arms to face the congregation, the pastor shall say: I now present to you Mr. and Mrs. _____ (groom's full name).

Recessional

Mark Corts, Pastor
Calvary Baptist Church
Winston-Salem, North Carolina

Ceremony 4

Processional

Introduction

Because the image of God indwells us, we are able to know and personally experience love. It has been said, "He that abideth in love, abideth in God." This is a realization which is celebrated in worship. Where there is the presence of love, there should be worship, for God is the author of love, and He is the Holy One we worship. Therefore, it is the heartfelt desire of _____ (groom) and _____ (bride) to welcome you— to welcome you to share and celebrate their covenant and commitment of love during this time of worship.

In the past (time period), _____ (groom) and _____ (bride) have learned to know and to love each other. Now they have decided to live their lives together as husband and wife.

We have been invited to hear _____ (groom) and _____ (bride) as they promise to face the future together, accepting whatever may lie ahead. These surroundings were not chosen by chance, just as _____ (groom) and _____ (bride) believe that they did not meet by chance. They believe that God directed them to be in the same place at the same time, and that it was God's will that helped them to find each other. For the beauty around us, for the strength it offers, and for the peace it brings, we are grateful.

_____ (groom) and _____ (bride), nothing is easier than saying words, and nothing harder than living them day after day. What you promise now must be renewed and redecided tomorrow. At the end of this ceremony, legally you will be man and wife, but you still decide, each day that stretches out before you, you want to be married.

Real love is something beyond the warmth and glow, the excitement and romance of being deeply in love. It is caring as much about the welfare and happiness of your marriage partner as about your own. But real love is not total absorption in each other; it is looking outward in the same direction together. Love makes burdens lighter, because you divide them. It makes joys more intense, because you share them. It makes you stronger, so you can reach out and become involved with life in ways you dared not risk alone.

Dear family and friends, having gathered in this beautiful place for the purpose of solemnizing the sacred rites of matrimony, who gives this woman to this man in wedlock?

Response: (Usually by father of the bride or other designated man) Her mother and I.

(The father (or other designee) then takes the right hand of the bride and places it in the right hand of the groom, and then he returns to be seated. The minister then takes his place in the pulpit behind a kneeling rail if possible, nods for the couple to come up before him and for the best man and maid of honor to take their places on either side. Then the wedding ceremony begins.)

Ceremony

Holy and happy is the sacred hour in which two devoted hearts are joined in the bonds of matrimony. Here in our swelling breasts we are reminded of the myriad, magic charm of home, of the quiet fireside, where Christ and His peace that passeth all understanding are the respected, the cherished, and the permanent guests. Here we are reminded of the lengthening days when the eventide shadows are fringed with the silver of devoted companion-ship's purest sympathy.

Originating in divine wisdom and goodness, designed to promote human happiness and ho-liness, this rite is the foundation of home life and social order and must remain so until the end of time. It was sanctioned and honored by the presence in power of our Savior at the mar-riage in Cana of Galilee and marked the begin-ning of His wondrous works.

Marriage is of God. It is ordained of heaven. It is the first and the holiest institution among men. God Himself gave the first bride away. God Himself performed the first wedding cere-mony. In the garden of Eden our Heavenly Father Himself hallowed and sanctified the first home. In the wisdom of the Almighty, the first establishment is not the church, it is not of the state, it is not of the schools; it is of the home the Lord God first speaks:

"And the Lord God took the man [whom He had made], and put him into the garden of Eden. . . . And the Lord God said, It is not good that the man should be alone; I will make him an help meet for him . . . And the Lord caused a deep sleep to fall upon Adam, and he slept; and he took one of his ribs, and closed up the flesh instead thereof; And the rib, which the Lord God had taken from man, made he a woman, and brought her unto the man. And Adam said, This is now bone of my bones, and flesh of my flesh; she shall be called Woman, because she was taken out of Man. Therefore shall a man leave his father and his mother, and shall cleave unto his wife: and they shall be one flesh" (Gen. 2:15,18,21-24).

From that beautiful, Edenic day of purity and innocence until this present moment, in the strong love of a man for his wife, and in the love and reverence of a wife for her husband, we have found our highest hope and our sweetest promise for a fairer day.

Marriage and home are built upon the foundation of the sublimest dedication known to the human heart—that of unselfish love and heavenly affection. With many tears and deep searching of heart, giving up her native home and country and people, Ruth spoke of that dedication in these immortal words: "Intreat me not to leave thee, or to return from following after thee: for whither thou goest, I will go; and where thou lodgest I will lodge: thy people shall be my people, and thy God my God. Where thou diest, will I die, and there will I be buried: the Lord do so to me, and more also, if aught but death part thee and me" (Ruth 1:16-17).

The apostle Paul spoke of that devotion like this: "Though I speak with the tongues of men and of angels, and have not charity [love], I am become as sounding brass or a tinkling [clanging] cymbal. And though I have the gift of prophecy, and understand all mysteries, and all knowledge; and though I have all faith, so that I could remove mountains, and have not [love], I am nothing. And though I bestow all my goods to feed the poor, and though I give my body to be burned, and have not [love], it profiteth me nothing. [Love] suffereth long and is kind; [love] envieth not, . . . seeketh not her own, is not easily provoked, . . . Beareth all things. . . . [Love] never faileth: but whether there be prophecies, they shall fail; whether there be tongues, they shall cease, whether there be knowledge, it shall vanish away. . . . Now abideth faith, hope, charity [love], these three; but the greatest of these is charity [love]" (1 Cor. 13:1-13).

The same inspired apostle Paul wrote on the sacred page:

> Wives, submit yourselves unto your husbands, as unto the Lord. For the husband is the head of the wife, even as Christ is the head of the church! . . . Therefore, as the church is subject unto Christ, so let the wives be to their own husbands in everything. Husbands, love your wives, even as Christ also loved the church and gave him-

self for it . . . So ought men to love their wives as their own bodies . . . For we are members of his body, of his flesh, and of his bones. For this cause shall a man leave his father and mother, and shall be joined unto his wife, and they two shall be one flesh. This is a great mystery . . . (see Eph. 5:22-32).

And it is a great mystery—how God can take two hearts and two lives and make them one is a great mystery, a mystery of heaven, but one that will be a strength and a blessing to you both as long as time shall last.

Vows

Realizing, therefore, the sacredness and the sanctity of the holy covenant you now make with each other, if you know of no barrier to such a union between yourselves, you will signify such by joining your right hands.

Do you, _____ (groom), in the presence of God and these assembled witnesses, promise to love and to cherish, in sickness and in health, in prosperity and in adversity, this woman whose right hand you now hold? Do you promise to be to her in all things a true and faithful husband, to cleave unto her, and to her only, as long as life shall last?

Response: I do.

Do you take her to be your lawful, wedded wife, as long as you both shall live? Do you?

Response: I do.

Do you, _____ (bride), in the presence of God and these assembled witnesses, promise to love and to cherish, in sickness and in health, in prosperity and in adversity, this young man whose right hand you now hold? Do you promise to be to him in all things a true and faithful wife, to cleave unto him, and to him only, as long as life shall last? Do you?

Response: I do.

Do you take him to be your lawfully, wedded husband, as long as you both shall live? Do you?

Response: I do.

_____ (Groom), do you possess a token of your love and affection to give to your bride, a seal of this holy covenant?

Response: I do.

What is it?

Response: A ring.

In all ages and among all peoples, the ring has been a symbol of that which is measureless; and thus, in this holy hour, a symbol of your measureless, boundless devotion. It is a circle; it has neither beginning nor ending; so down to old age and death and forever you are to keep this vow inviolate, and the sign and the seal

thereof will be this ring. As a ceaseless reminder of this sacred committal, place this ring
on the wedding finger of your bride and repeat
after me.

I, _____ (groom), take thee, _____
(bride), to my wedded wife, to have and to hold
from this day forward, for richer for poorer, for
better for worse, to cleave unto thee, and to thee
only, as long as we both shall live. With this ring
I thee wed, with loyal love I thee endow, all my
worldly goods with thee I share, in the name of
the Father, and of the Son, and of the Holy
Spirit, blessed forevermore. Amen.

_____ (bride), do you possess a token of
your love and affection, to give your husband, a
seal of this holy covenant?

Response: I do.

What is it?

Response: A ring.

Invested with the same significance as the
ring you have just received, a circle of precious
gold indicating the longevity of your love and
the pricelessness of your devotion, place this
ring on the wedded finger of your husband and
repeat after me.

I, _____ (bride), take thee, _____
(groom), to my wedded husband, to have and
to hold, from this day forward, for richer for
poorer, for better for worse, to cleave unto thee,

and to thee only, as long as we both shall live. With this ring I thee wed, with all the loyal love of my heart I thee endow, in the name of the blessed Trinity, the Father, the Son, and the Holy Spirit. Amen.

Pronouncement

And now by the virtue of the authority invested in me as a minister of the gospel of Christ Jesus our Lord, and as the pastor of this beloved church, in the presence of God and these assembled witnesses, I pronounce you husband and wife, no longer two but one, one in interest, in destiny, in love, and in life.

And upon you, _____ (groom) and upon you, _____ (bride), his helpmate in all his work, may heaven's richest benedictions ever abide, making you a blessing to all who shall ever know and love you. To that end let us pray.

Prayer

Benediction

May almighty God, with His word of blessing, untie your hearts in the never-ending bond of pure love.

May your children bring you happiness, and may your generous love for them be returned to you many times over.

May the peace of Christ live always in your hearts and in your home. May you have true friends to stand by you, both in joy and in sorrow. May you be ready and willing to help and comfort all who come to you in need. And may the blessings promised to the compassionate be yours in abundance.

May you find happiness and satisfaction in your work. May daily problems never cause you undue anxiety, nor the desire for earthly possessions dominate your lives. But may our heart's first desire be always for the good things waiting for you in the life of heaven.

May the Lord bless you with many happy years together, so that you may enjoy the rewards of a good life. And after you have served Him loyally in His kingdom on earth, may He welcome you to His eternal kingdom in heaven.

And may Almighty God bless you, in the name of the Father, and the Son, and the Holy Spirit. Amen.

Recessional

Suggested Alternatives in the Ceremony

There is no end to the variety that can be achieved in a wedding ceremony. For example, during the first part of the ceremony the beautiful sonnet of Elizabeth Barrett Browning writ-

ten to her husband Robert Browning can be
added:

> How do I love thee? Let me count the
> ways.
> I love thee to the depth and breadth and
> height
> My soul can reach, when feeling out of
> sight
> For the ends of Being and ideal Grace;
> I love thee to the level of everyday's
> Most quiet need, by sun and
> candle-light.
> I love thee freely, as men strive for Right;
> I love thee purely, as they turn from
> Praise;
> I love thee with the passion put to use
> In my old griefs, and with my
> childhood's faith.
> I love thee with a love I seemed to lose
> With my lost saints,—I love thee with the
> breath,
> Smiles, tears, of all my life!—and if God
> choose,
> I shall but love thee better after death.

Ring Vows Spoken Simultaneously

With this ring, we pledge our love together, to
Christ and to His church, even as He loved the
church and gave Himself for it. We ask His

blessings upon the home we build in His name and the sign and the seal of that Christian commitment in this golden wedding band that binds us to each other and to our Savior forever.

In the name of the Father and of the Son and of the Holy Spirit. Amen.

The Unity Candle

One way to use a unity candle is to place a three-branched candlestick by the side of the pastor with the center candle unlighted. After the pastor pronounces the couple husband and wife, they then each take a lighted candle, set aflame the one in the middle, blow out each his and her candle, leaving the one in the center lighted. The pastor then asks the husband to kiss his wife, and then leave together while the recessional is being played.

Another way to use a unity candle is to place three candles on one stand at the front of the sanctuary. Before the groom's mother is seated, she with her accompanying husband light one of the candles. Before the bride's mother is seated, she and her accompanying husband light the candle on the other side, leaving the one in the center unlighted. After the ceremony, the bride and groom step down from the pulpit and before proceeding out of the church each takes one of the candles (the groom the one his parents lighted, the bride the one her parents lighted), light the candle in the middle, then blowing out the light each one holds, replaces them in their holders, leaving the one large candle burning in the center.

Another way of using the unity candle is for the pastor to call the two sets of parents to stand before him and the unity candle as he says:

Life without love is like a tree without blossom and fruit. So it is now, that we turn for a moment to the parents of these two who have given so much love through the years. It must be a particular pleasure and a great satisfaction for these parents, _____ and _____ (groom's parents), _____ and _____ (bride's parents), as they stand here with _____ (groom) and _____ (bride). You have watched them mature physically and helped them to mature spiritually. You have watched with love and affection as they have entered into this relationship with each other. You have cried, laughed, consoled, and been consoled, desired for, and realized many wishes come true from within your parental relationship. You have prayed many prayers and provided the guidance that has helped them to become the responsible Christian adults they are today. You have expressed your love in so many ways through the years as once again you do so now by standing beside them as they establish a home that will be so much stronger because of the Christian homes which they have known personally.

Who then, having played such an important role in helping these two become the persons they are, now promise their prayers and blessings to the formation of this new home?

Parents respond: We do.

The parents then light their candle, and the pastor goes to his place at the pulpit.

Postscript

However and whatever the ceremony and order of the wedding, the service is to be deeply religious, Christian, and spiritual. People ought to feel that they have "been to church," especially the bride, the groom, and their families.

Remember, the building of the Christian home is one of the most important foundations in realizing the kingdom of God on earth. There is no such thing as a Christian church without a Christian home and the home actually begins in the wedding covenant.

> W. A. Criswell, Senior Pastor
> First Baptist Church
> Dallas, Texas

From W. A. Criswell, *Criswell's Guidebook for Pastors* (Nashville: Broadman Press, 1980), 285-291. Used by permission.

Ceremony 5

Processional

Introduction

Today we have gathered in this beautiful sanctuary to join _____ (groom) and _____ (bride) in the bonds of holy marriage and in a special way to give honor and glory to our Lord Jesus Christ.

In God's great love and wisdom, He instituted the first home. It did not originate in the heart and mind of man but in the heart and mind of God. There is no human relationship that can compare to that of husband and wife. We stand with a sense of awe and reverence as we come to this altar tonight.

Pledge of Parents of Both Bride and Groom

(Parents of both bride and groom stand.)

_____ you and _____ (bride's parents) have carefully and lovingly provided for

_____ (bride) over these years. Blessed indeed is the woman who has loving and caring parents. Only a father and mother can fully understand the meaning of parental love. You have provided for her wisely and compassionately all of her life and with loving care you have prepared her for this step of marriage.

_____, do you and _____ (bride's parents) give your permission for the joining together of _____ (bride) and _____ (groom)?

Answer: We do.

Do you joyfully and faithfully pledge your prayers to them in this marriage?

Answer: We do. And will you receive _____ (groom) as your very own son and pledge to love him as you do _____ (bride)?

Answer: We do.

Now, do you _____ and _____ (groom's parents) give your approval and blessing to _____ (groom) and _____ (bride) through your faithful love and dedication? Do you now receive _____ (bride) as your very own daughter and pledge your love and devotion to her as she joins your family circle?

Answer: We do.

(Each of the fathers will then have opportunity to lead in a prayer of dedication).

Exchange of Rings

As a sign and a symbol of your commitment
to each other, you have selected a ring of gold.
The ring is one of the signs of marriage in our
culture. The ring does not make you married,
but it reveals you to be married. It is much more
than a piece of jewelry. It is not an ornament or a
trinket, but it shares the special message that
you belong to each other. It represents your
vows and commitment to each other. It symbolizes in so many ways what you say to each other
today and each day that you live. The ring is
made of the purest metal. Few metals are more
treasured than gold. The ring from this precious
metal is a fitting symbol of the precious nature
of your love. It also expresses the purity of the
love you give to each other and will keep each
for the other.

The ring is a circle, never starting and never
ending. This is a symbol of the fact that you
pledge a love that is endless. Not even death
will break the love you cherish for each other.
The ring has always had an important place in
the relationships of mankind. When history
was young and the state new, the power of an
empire was vested in the signet ring worn by
the ruling monarch. All that was required for a

treaty, an agreement, a purchase, or a law to be permanent, legal and binding was the imprint of that ring upon the document. From earliest times rings have often been given as a token of friendship and enduring good will. But in our day the rings are used for the most beautiful reason of all: sealing the engagement and marriage vows.

This ring represents authority and power in an extraordinary manner. God has given you, in your home, authority and power as husband and wife, keepers of the home and givers of life as God directs. The ring tells a special story of the commitments you have made to each other.

I pray that these rings will be a reminder to you of these truths and your commitment. More than that, I pray that the rings will be a testimony of your faithfulness to the vows you have made today.

Do you _____ (groom), give this ring to _____ (bride) as a token of your love for her?

Answer: I do.

Will you, _____ (bride), wear this ring as evidence of your love for _____ (groom)?

Answer: I will.

Will you now face each other? _____ (groom), place this ring on _____ (bride's) left hand, holding it there, and repeat after me.

I, _____ (groom), take thee _____ (bride) to my wedded wife, to have and to hold from this day forward, for better or worse, for richer or poorer, in sickness and in health, in the good that might brighten your ways, in the sadness that may darken your days, to love and cherish till death do us part, according to God's holy ordinance and thereto I give you my love.

Do you _____ (bride) give this ring to _____ (groom) as a token of your love for him?

Answer: I do.

Will you _____ (groom) wear this ring as evidence of your love for _____ (bride)?

Answer: I will.

_____ (bride), place this ring on _____ (groom's) finger, holding it there, and repeat after me. I _____ (bride) take thee _____ (groom) to my wedded husband, to have and to hold, from this day forward, for better or worse, for richer or poorer, in sickness and in health, in the good that may brighten our ways, in the sadness that may darken our days, to love and cherish, till death do us part, according to God's holy ordinance and thereto I give you my love.

You have now pledged your lives to each other. I would remind you that only as you faithfully accept the responsibilities that are involved in this new relationship will you find true and lasting happiness. I would like to require you to walk often down memory's lane. Just remember. Remember the occasion of your meeting, the days of your friendship and your courtship. Remember all the details that went into making this occasion a reality. Remember all these friends and loved ones who have come to share, some from many miles, because they love you and care about you. The memory of all these things will be a source of encouragement, blessing, and happiness to you in the years that are ahead. Most of all, remember that the vows you have given have been given unto God as well as to each other.

The Pronouncement

It has been a joy for me to share these moments with you. Looking to God for divine sanction, and by the authority vested in me by this state as a minister of the gospel, I pronounce you husband and wife, henceforth, in interest, in affection, in purpose as in destiny, one. What God hath joined together, let no man put asunder (see Mark 10:9).

Prayer

Kiss

Recessional

James T. Draper, Jr., Pastor
First Baptist Church
Euless, Texas

Ceremony 6

Processional

Introduction

I welcome everyone here to this special occasion in the lives of _____ (bride) and _____ (groom). We are here to worship Jesus Christ through the institution called the wedding ceremony between _____ (bride) and _____ (groom). I now ask this very important question, Who gives this bride in marriage?

Response: Her mother and I.

Ephesians 5:31 says, "For this cause a man shall leave his father and mother and shall cleave to his wife; and the two shall become one flesh." The Scriptures speak of the oneness that you two shall have after this wedding ceremony. The admonition to you, _____ (bride) and to you _____ (groom) is to *leave* and to *cleave*. You are to leave your parents and cleave together in your new family. I challenge you to think about three matters before you take your vows together and to God.

First, I challenge you to be one in your commitment to God. You will not make it together for a lifetime unless you are both committed in like faith to Jesus Christ. Marriage is a spiritual experience. The ultimate priority of each of your lives should be your personal commitment to and your walk with Jesus Christ. Be one in your commitment to God.

Second, I want you to be one in your commitment to each other. The Bible points out clearly the need to leave your parents and cleave to one another. Your commitment should be willfully, sacrificially, and unconditionally to accept and love each other. This type of commitment is a must for your marriage to be a success.

Third, I strongly urge you to be one in your commitment to your future. Your future does not belong to you, but to Jesus Christ because He is your Lord. I encourage you to allow Him to lead you throughout your entire lives. If commitment to His will for your future together is decided upon now, then you will be in oneness with Christ and with each other. Be one in your commitment to your future together.

Prayer

Dear Father, what a joy it is to observe a man and a woman so much in love with you and each other. Bless them with your strength now as they verbalize these commitments to you and to each other. May these commitments bring glory to your Son, Jesus Christ. Amen.

Vows

_____ (bride) and _____ (groom), if you are ready to make these vows to God and to each other, please step forward, turn toward one another, and join hands.

_____ (groom), would you please repeat these words after me if they are the desire of your heart? I, _____ (groom), take thee, _____ (bride), to be my wedded wife, to have and to hold from this day forward, for better, for worse, for richer, for poorer, in sickness and in health, to love, and to cherish till death do us part; and to you I pledge my faithfulness.

_____ (bride), would you please repeat these words after me if they are the desire of your heart: I, _____ (bride), take thee, _____ (groom), to be my wedded husband, to have and to hold from this day forward, for better, for worse, for richer, for poorer, in sickness and in health, to love, to cherish, and to obey, till death do us part; and to you I pledge my faithfulness.

Exchange of Rings

Each of you have rings for the other. Would you exchange them? (As they are exchanging rings, the pastor says the following words:) As a ceaseless reminder of this hour, and of the promise you have made to each other and to Jesus Christ, you place a ring on your loved one's finger. It is symbolic of your pledge and faith. It is given and received in the name of Jesus Christ, and it reinforces your faith and love to each other. The rings also speak of the oneness you now experience as husband and wife. Would you please kneel as we pray?

Prayer

Unity Candle

In order to symbolize the oneness you have together you will now light the unity candle. (Music is played as the bride and groom light the candle and make their way back to stand before the pastor.)

Pronouncement

_____ (groom) and _____ (bride), by the authority given to me by the Lord Jesus Christ as a pastor of one of His churches, and by the authority invested in me as a licensed and ordained minister of the gospel, I pronounce you husband and wife. _____ (groom), you may now kiss your wife.

As soon as the kiss is over the couple faces the congregation, and the pastor says the following: Ladies and gentleman, it is my privilege to present to you Mr. and Mrs. _____ (groom's full name).

Recessional

Following the recessional, the pastor says the following: I want to thank you for being here. May God bless you.

> Ronnie Floyd, Pastor
> First Baptist Church
> Springdale, Arkansas

Ceremony 7

Processional

Welcome

We are happy to greet you today in the name of our Spiritual Bridegroom, the Lord Jesus Christ.

In behalf of the couple to be married today, I thank you for your presence. You came at their invitation, and your presence symbolizes your love for them, as well as your support for their future together. As their loved ones and friends, the most important contribution we can make to their marriage is to pray for them with warmth and consistency. Be prayerful, then, throughout this service and join me in a commitment of this marriage to the One who conceived marriage and who designed the home to have priority in all human relationships.

To think of marriage is to prompt thoughts of love. Yet, because there are so many misconceptions of love, it is needful to qualify the love upon which a home should be built.

Infatuation, misnamed love, is not adequate. Lust, misrepresented as love, is an enemy, not a friend of marriage.

Scripture

At this point we need a clear picture of love, trustworthy enough to venture into a life-long commitment of marriage. There is just such a picture of love portrayed in the thirteenth chapter of 1 Corinthians.

If I speak with the tongues of men and of angels, but do not have love, I have become a noisy gong or a clanging cymbal. And if I have the gift of prophecy, and know all mysteries and all knowledge; and if I have all faith, so as to remove mountains, but do not have love, I am nothing. And if I give all my possessions to feed the poor, and if I deliver my body to be burned, but do not love, it profits me nothing. Love is patient, love is kind, and is not jealous; love does not brag and is not arrogant, does not act unbecomingly; it does not seek its own, is not provoked, does not take into account a wrong suffered, does not rejoice in unrighteousness, but rejoices with the truth; bears all things, believes all things, hopes all things, endures all things. Love never fails; but if there are gifts of prophecy, they will be done away; if there are tongues, they will cease; if there is knowledge, it will be done away. For we know in part, and we prophesy in part; but when the perfect comes, the partial will be done away. When I was a child, I used to speak as a child, think as a child, reason as a child; but when I became a man, I did away with childish things. For now we see in a mirror dimly, but then face to face; now I know in part, but then I shall know fully just as I also have been fully known. But now abide faith, hope, love, these three; but the greatest of these is love (NASB).

And the greatest love about which we know is the love that sent the Lord Jesus Christ to Calvary to shed His blood for our salvation. We trust you know the Lord Jesus as your personal Savior, for to be committed to Him is to be numbered among those whose joy it is to be called the Bride of Christ.

Now we invite you to join with this dedicated couple in the worship of the Lord and in the establishment of their home which is to honor Him.

Processional

Prayer

_____ (groom) and _____ (bride), I want to thank you for inviting us to share this occasion with you today. We are here to assure you of our love and our prayerful support throughout the years to come.

I commend you for your wedding plans and your approach to marriage. There are those in our day who ridicule traditional values, scoff at the idea of purity at the wedding altar, and even contend that marriage, as we have known it, is passé to a forward-thinking society.

I remind you that such a being as a perfectly created man could not enjoy the environment of a perfectly created Eden without the companionship of a kindred heart. Hence, God provided Eve to be Adam's companion and his ever-new delight. God viewed them in their happiness, and He, in the sovereign sense, pronounced them husband and wife.

So marriage is of divine initiative. It is the design of God's mind, and it is His conception. It is so sacred that God has ordained that death, and death only, should sever those He unites in marriage.

When we read the concluding words of the creation account, we suddenly realize that marriage is, in a real sense, the completion of the creation act.

"Therefore shall a man leave his father and mother, and shall cleave unto his wife: and they shall be one flesh" (Gen. 2:24).

The two of you, then, become the rest of each other in marriage. You are individuals, with distinct roles, gifts, and responsibilities, yet you are, together, a completed creation, an entity of God's design.

I charge you, then, to be an example of all God had in mind when He conceived the home. Be a source of encouragement to those who contemplate marriage in their future. Silence the critics of marriage by the witness of your own happiness. Allow your home to illustrate the truth of the church's relationship to Christ, and let the Lord rejoice in His observation of your fulfillment.

Vows

_____ (groom), will you promise before God, before me, His minister, and before these, your loved ones and friends, that throughout the remainder of your life, your preeminent allegiance will belong to Jesus Christ, and your first earthly love will belong to your mate?

Response: I will.

_____ (bride,) will you promise before God, before me, His minister, and before these, your loved ones and friends, that throughout the remainder of your life, your preeminent allegiance will belong to Jesus Christ, and your first earthly love will belong to your mate?

Response: I will.

_____ (groom), will you then receive this woman to be your wedded wife, to live together after God's plan for marriage; will you love her, honor, cherish, and keep her, and forsaking all others, will you keep only to her so long as you may live?

Response: I will.

_____ (bride), will you then receive this man to be your wedded husband, to live together after God's plan for marriage; will you love him, honor, cherish, and keep him, and forsaking all others, will you keep only unto him so long as you may live?

Response: I will.

We rejoice with you today in the presence of your family members. They are an intricate part of this occasion. Your parents take joy in your arrival at this moment in your lives. They have loved you, prayed for you, shared many anxious moments over you, dreamed for you, listened to you, affirmed you, and have believed God in your behalf.

Because they are such a vital part of your lives and seek to support you in the establishment of your own home, I would ask, Who gives this woman to be wed to this man?

Response (usually the bride's father): Her mother and I.

Before you exchange vows with each other, I remind you of the clear, reasonable instruction God has provided us regarding the roles of husband and wife: "Wives, be subject to your own husbands, as to the Lord. For the husband is the head of the wife, as Christ also is the head of the church, He Himself being the Savior of the body" (Eph. 5:22-23, NASB).

Vows

I, _____ (groom), receive you, _____ (bride), to my wedded wife, to have and hold from this day forward, for better or worse, for richer or poorer, in sickness and health, to love and to cherish, 'til death do us part. And, hitherto, I pledge you my faith in the name of the Father, the Son, and the Holy Spirit.

I, _____ (bride), receive you, _____ (groom), to my wedded husband, to have and hold from this day forward, for better or worse, for richer or poorer, in sickness and health, to love and to cherish, 'til death do us part. And, hitherto, I pledge you my faith in the name of the Father, the Son, and the Holy Spirit.

Ring Ceremony

_____ (groom), what token do you have today as a symbol of your marriage?

Response: A ring.

_____ (bride), what token do you have to-day as a symbol of your marriage?

Response: A ring.

Before you exchange these rings, and share in a ring pledge, let me remind you that they symbolize the love you have experienced which God has for you. Thus you can understand the love you should have for each other.

A ring is a circle, with no place of ending. It symbolizes a love between you which shall never cease. Your rings are made of gold, the least tarnishable of all metals, symbolizing the love between you which will never grow old.

Place these rings upon each other's left hand and, together, share this ring pledge in unison: As a pledge, and in token of vows between us made, with this ring, I thee wed.

(At this point the unity candle may be used, lighting the center candle and dowsing the two outside candles. At this time the pastor quotes Ephesians 5:31.) "For this cause shall a man leave his father and mother, and shall be joined unto his wife, and they two shall be one flesh."

The couple kneels, joining hands, and the pastor prays, pronouncing them husband and wife as part of the prayer.

Recessional

> Charles G. Fuller, Pastor
> First Baptist Church
> Roanoke, Virginia

Ceremony 8

Processional

Introduction

Dearly beloved, we are gathered together in the presence of God and of these assembled witnesses to join together this man and this woman in bonds of holy matrimony. Sacred and happy is this hour when two hearts bound together by the enchanting ties of marital love come to this altar, but that hour is even more sacred and happier still when the two contracting parties come in reverence toward God in faith in our Lord Jesus and indwelled by His Holy Spirit, the seal of every believer.

It is our confession that the first ceremony was witnessed by the angels of heaven and was officiated by God Himself in the garden of Eden as the first man and the first woman were bound together in the ties of marital love. Our Lord Jesus Christ made a wedding at Cana, a village in Galilee, the occasion for His first great sign and miracle in John's Gospel, and by His attendance He set forever His seal of approval on this relationship. Perhaps it reached its highest pinnacle of significance when the apostle Paul, guided by the Holy Spirit, made the relationship between a husband and a wife the emblematic symbol of that relationship between Christ and His church.

We believe that the Word of God has given to us not only the permission but also the pattern for this relationship. The apostle Paul, writing to the church at Corinth, reminded them that if we speak in the tongues of men and of angels but have not love, we are as a resounding gong or a clanging cymbal. If we have the gift of prophecy and can fathom all mystery and all knowledge, and if we have faith that can move mountains, but have not love, we are nothing. If we give all we possess to the poor and surrender our body to the flames but have not love, we am nothing (see 1 Cor. 1:1-3).

He follows that by giving fourteen characteristics of love. The home is the laboratory of love. "Love is patient, love is kind, it does not envy, it does not boast. It is not proud, it is not rude, it is not self seeking, it is not easily angered, it keeps no record of wrong. Love does not delight in evil but rejoices with the truth. It always pro-

tects, always trusts, always hopes, always perseveres (1 Cor. 13:4-8*a*, NIV).

Our Lord Jesus predicted that a time would
come when a man and a woman would leave
father and mother and cleave to each other, and
being joined together, they would become one
flesh. So, on His authority I ask, Who gives this
woman to this man to be wed?

Response (usually father of the bride): Her
mother and I.

Vows

The two of you have come to me signifying
your desire to be joined together in holy matrimony. Being assured that no grounds exist to
hinder this union, may we bow together in
prayer as we ask God's blessings on these vows
and exchange of physical tokens?

Prayer

Our Heavenly Father, we come, our hearts
filled with thanksgiving, for the divine provision that You have made for us in Your original
insights and pronouncement that it is not good
for man to be alone. Rather, You have made us
to find our highest fulfillment together in You.
We thank You for the homes and the heritage
represented here as _____ (groom's name)

and _____ (bride's name) stand together in this hour. We thank You for every act of care, nurture, sacrifice, provision, and love that has been shown to them by those who have loved them and nurtured them even to this hour. But now we recognize, Father, that something new is about to happen. As You have instructed, it is time for them to leave their first loyalty to other families and cleave to each other so that from this day forward it will be one for the other, sealed by thy blessings, spirit, and love that will be the manifest reality of their life together.

We pray that these vows being exchanged, these tokens of love that are given one to the other, might ever remain sacred and may we be reminded that beyond these visible witnesses, these words spoken are witnessed by heaven itself and sealed by the presence of thy Holy Spirit. Dear Father, we pray your blessings upon this home You founded, this union that is here promised, for we ask it in Jesus' name and for His divine purpose. Amen.

Vows

You have come, this evening, to exchange your vows, one to the other. And I will ask you _____ (groom) to repeat after me these vows as you pledge your promise to _____ (bride).

I, _____ (groom), take you _____ (bride) to be my lawful and wedded wife, to have and to hold from this day forward forever, in sickness as well as in health, in poverty as well as in wealth, in the good that lights your days or the bad that darkens your ways, and to be true to you alone 'til death alone parts us. I do so promise.

And now, _____ (bride), taking the man who holds you by the hand to be your lawful and wedded husband, I ask you to repeat these vows after me. I, _____ (bride), take you, _____ (groom), to be my lawful and wedded husband. From this day forward and forever, in sickness as well as in health, in poverty as well as in wealth, in the good that lights our days or the bad that darkens our ways, and to be true to you alone until death only shall part us. I do so promise.

The two of you are devoted one to the other by the exchange of these marital vows in the sight of these witnesses and the Triune God.

Exchange of Rings

Now the two of you wish to indicate the lifelong nature of this union, its purity and its fidelity by the exchange of wedding rings. Lost sometime in earliest history of mankind is the beginning of the significance of a ring. We do know that from time immemorial it was used to seal prestigious documents. We also know it was used to guarantee the integrity of any document, but when it comes to the wedding altar it reaches a pinnacle of significance, for from here it is the circular form never ending which indicates the quality of your commitment and love to each other and the purity of its metal indicates the purity and the fidelity of your love one for the other.

_____ (groom), will you give this ring to _____ (bride) as a token and an emblem of her love for you as well as yours for her?

Groom: I will.

_____ (bride), will you take this ring and wear it as a token and an emblem of _____ (groom) love for you as well as yours for him?

Bride: I will.

Taking this ring _____ (bride), will you give it to _____ (groom) as a token of his love for you as well as a token of your love for him?

Bride: I will.

_____ (groom), in taking this ring that _____ (bride) gives to you, will you take it and wear it both as an emblem of your love for her as well as her love for you?

Groom: I will.

Now, by the exchange of these visible tokens,

wedding rings, you do make manifest the vows that you have spoken from this day forward forever.

Pronouncement

And now, having asked God's blessings on these vows and promises thus spoken, and having heard your recital of these promises one to the other, and witnessed the exchange of these tokens of your love, under the laws of this state—but more than that, under the higher sanction of the kingdom of God—I now pronounce you to be husband and wife. What God has joined together, let not man put asunder (see Mark 10:9). And may I be the first to present to you Mr. and Mrs. _____ (groom's full name).

Recessional

> Joel C. Gregory, Pastor
> First Baptist Church
> Dallas, Texas

Ceremony 9

Processional

Introduction

We welcome you to this ceremony as a celebration of love. Marriage is God's truest celebration of love. In 1 Corinthians 13 we read:

> Love is patient, love is kind, and is not jealous; Love does not brag and is not arrogant, does not act unbecomingly; it does not seek its own, is not provoked, does not take into account a wrong suffered, does not rejoice in unrighteousness, but rejoices with the truth; bears all things, believes all things, hopes all things, endures all things. Love never fails (vv. 4-8a, NASB).

Paul concludes that chapter by saying, "But now abide faith, hope, love, these three; but the greatest of these is love" (v. 13, NASB). Love demands a mutual submission, as Paul says in Ephesians 5:20-21, "always giving thanks for all

things in the name of our Lord Jesus Christ to
God, even the Father; and be subject to one another in the fear of Christ" (NASB).

He speaks a word to the wives.

> Wives, be subject to your own hus-
> bands, as to the Lord. For the husband is
> the head of the wife, as Christ also is the
> head of the church, He Himself being the
> Savior of the body. But as the church is
> subject to Christ, so also the wives ought
> to be to their husbands in everything (Eph.
> 5:22-24, NASB).

Then he speaks a word of encouragement
and definition to the husband:

> Husbands, love your wives, just as
> Christ also loved the church and gave
> Himself up for her. So husbands ought
> also to love their wives as their own
> bodies. He who loves his own wife loves
> himself; for no one ever hated his own
> flesh, but nourishes and cherishes it, just
> as Christ also does the church.
>
> For this cause a man shall leave his
> father and mother, shall cleave to his wife;
> and the two shall become one flesh. Never-
> theless let each individual among you also
> love his own wife even as himself; and let

the wife see to it that she respect her husband (Eph. 5:25,28-29,31,33, NASB).

The wife's role is that of an attitude of reverence in her spirit, a servant's heart, a grateful
spirit, and a quiet spirit. The role of the husband
is to be that of a priest to lead his family in worship, a provider to furnish for them the necessi-
ties of life and a protector from both physical
and spiritual evils.

If the two of you believe this to be the will of
God and stand ready to receive each other publicly as a gift from God, with perfections and
imperfections alike, join your right hands.

Vows

_____ (groom), in taking this woman you
hold by the right hand to be your lawful and
wedded wife, before God and the witnesses
present, you must promise to love her, to honor
and cherish her in that relation, and leaving all
others cleave only unto her, and be to her in all
things a true and faithful husband so long as
you both shall live.

Response: I do.

_____ (bride), in taking this man you
hold by the right hand to be your lawful and
wedded husband, before God and the witness
present, you must promise to love him, to

honor and cherish him in that relation, and leaving all others cleave only until him, and be to him in all things a true and faithful wife so long as you both shall live.

Response: I do.

Then are you each given to the other for richer or poorer, for better or worse, in sickness or in health, til death shall part you.

Exchange of Rings

The circle of the ring stands for endless union which makes it a relationship of fidelity. _____ (groom), as a ceaseless reminder of this hour and the vows you both have taken, take this ring and place it upon the hand of _____ (bride) and repeat these vows after me. With this ring I thee wed. With loyal love I thee endow. And all my worldly goods with thee I share. In the name of the Father, Son, and Holy Spirit blessed forever more.

Now, _____ (bride), repeat after me: With this ring I thee wed. With loyal love I thee endow. And all my worldly goods with thee I share. In the name of the Father, Son, and Holy Spirit blessed forever more.

In the Book of Ruth we read: Behold, your sister-in-law has gone back to her people and her gods; return after your sister-in-law. But Ruth said, Do not urge me to leave you or turn back from following you; for where you go, I will go, and where you lodge, I will lodge. Your people shall be my people, and your God, my God (Ruth 1:15-16, NASB).

Prayer

Our Father, we thank You for having instituted divine matrimony and having established the family that provides us with human relationships that could not otherwise be experienced. It is our prayer at this moment that Your presence and power shall rest upon this couple, to keep them in times of difficulty, to sustain them in moments of abundance as well as in the moments of poverty. I pray You shall write these vows indelibly upon their hearts that they may walk with You and with each other and their love may grow for each other in proportion as their love grows in You. In Jesus' name we pray, Amen.

Pronouncement

Forasmuch as the two of you have covenanted together according to the teaching of the Scripture and laws of this state, and by the authority vested in me as an ordained minister, I hereby pronounce you husband and wife. "What God hath joined together, let not man put asunder" (Mark 10:9).

Recessional

> George M. Harris, Pastor
> Castle Hills Baptist Church
> San Antonio, Texas

Ceremony 10

Processional

Introduction

With great joy we come together to this holy place in the presence of our wonderful Lord and in the company of these witnesses to join together this man, _____ (groom), and this woman, _____ (bride), in holy matrimony. Marriage is commended by Paul to be honorable among all, and therefore it is not to be entered into unadvisedly or lightly, but reverently, discreetly, advisedly, and in the fear of God. Your presence here indicates your desire to establish a marital relationship, and we ask God to bless this occasion with His presence and to pave the pathway of this dear couple with His goodness and grace.

Who gives this woman to be married to this man?

Response: Her mother and I.

It is important for us to consider what God's

Word teaches about the marriage relationship. In the Holy Scriptures we are taught that marriage is a sacred institution established by God for the welfare of the race. In the beautiful and tranquil Garden of Eden, before the forbidden tree had yielded its fateful fruit, and before the tempter had touched the world, God saw that it was not good for man to be alone. He made a helpmate suitable for that first man, and He established the rite of marriage while the angels of heaven witnessed that wonderful scene.

In the Bible we are also taught that marriage was originated in the divine wisdom and goodness of God. It is designed to promote human happiness and holiness. This rite is the foundation of home life and social order and must be so until the end of time.

Marriage was sanctioned and honored by the presence and power of Jesus at the marriage feast in Cana of Galilee and marked the beginning of His miraculous works. It is declared, therefore, and so ordained, that a man shall leave his father and mother and cleave to his wife, and the two of them shall become one flesh—united in all of the hopes, aims, sentiments, and interests of this life.

In the Bible we are also taught that under the new covenant the marriage state has been sanctified to be a symbol of Christ and His church.

Therefore, the husband, as the head of the wife should love her even as Christ also loves the church. The wife also must be in subjection to her own husband in the Lord, even as the church is meant to be in subjection to Christ. Therefore, Christians thus united should love each other as one in the Lord, be faithful one to the other, assist each other mutually, and never forsake each other.

Prayer of Invocation

Dear Father in heaven, we desire to acknowledge you in all of our ways, that You may direct our steps. Especially do we need You in the great moments of life. Graciously regard Your servants who come before You to assume the mutual obligations involved in marriage. May they walk not heedlessly, but in holy reverence in the solemn step which they are about to take. Assure them and us of Your presence and let the beauty of our Lord Jesus Christ abide upon the celebration of this marriage. We humbly ask it in Jesus' name. Amen.

_____ (groom) and _____ (bride), I want to thank you for allowing me the opportunity to counsel with you concerning your marriage prior to this occasion. Our visits together have confirmed what I already knew. It is obvious to those of us who have heard your testimonies and seen your lives that you are devoted to the Lord Jesus Christ. You have both indicated to me that Jesus Christ is the Savior and Lord of your lives. Indeed, we know that Jesus Christ is the way, the truth, and the life and that no man cometh unto the Father but by Him. We know that Jesus said, I have come that you might have life and that you might have it more abundantly (see John 14:6; 10:10).

It is good to know that a bride and groom intend to bring into their newly established home the love of Christ, the power of a profound faith, the strength of an inflexible integrity, and the fruit of the Spirit of God. We are solemnly reminded by the apostle Paul that we should not be unequally yoked together with an unbeliever. I predict that you will experience profound joy in the future because God's Word says, "Except the Lord build the house, they labor in vain that build it." I know you are committed to allowing Christ to rule and reign in your home and to make it all that God would have it to be.

I would encourage you to establish a family altar so your home will become a place of worship. We realize that the first church was in a house. The Bible says that those early apostles went from house to house praising God and having fellowship one with another.

Let your own home be a house of prayer and a palace of praise. Continue to be faithful to the church and to let your spiritual light shine before men that they may see your good works and glorify the Father which is in heaven.

Vows

Let me also encourage you to remember that marriage is a covenant. The vows which you exchange should be shared without any selfish reservations, and they should be kept as a bond of honor. I believe that if you do this, your home will be an abiding joy and security to yourselves and a blessing to others.

_____ (groom), will you have this woman, _____ (bride), to be your wedded wife, to live together after God's ordinance in the holy estate of matrimony? Will you love her, honor her, and care for her, and through the grace of God prove yourself unto her in every respect a faithful Christian husband so long as you both shall live? If this is the desire of your heart, then answer I will.

Response: I will.

_____ (bride), will you have this man, _____ (groom), to be your wedded husband, to live together after God's ordinance in the holy estate of matrimony? Will you love him, honor him, and be subject unto him in the Lord, and through the grace of God prove yourself unto him in every respect a faithful Christian wife so long as you both shall live? If this is your desire, then answer I will.

Exchange of Rings

Now we come to the time for the giving and the receiving of the rings. From time immemorial, the ring has been used as an enduring evidence of good will and friendship. The golden circlet which is the most prized of all treasures has come to have its greatest prestige in the symbolic significance it vouches at the altar of marriage. Here untarnishable material and unique form become the precious tokens of the pure and abiding qualities of the ideal marital estate.

_____ (groom), place this ring upon _____ (bride's) finger and repeat after me: With this ring I thee wed. With loyal love I thee endow and all my worldly goods with thee I share, in the name of the Father, and the Son, and the Holy Spirit. Amen.

_____ (bride), place this ring upon _____ (groom's) finger and repeat after me:

With this ring I thee wed. With loyal love I thee
endow and all my worldly goods with thee I
share, in the name of the Father, and the Son,
and the Holy Spirit. Amen.

Prayer of Dedication

Dear Father in heaven, You have been a witness to what has taken place here. It is our re-
quest that you give to this bride and this groom
the spiritual strength to maintain the commitments which they have made here. Help them
to honor You in their individual lives and in the
home which they establish here this day. Crown
their marriage with Your grace and Your love
now and for as long as they both shall live. In
Jesus' name, Amen.

Lighting of Candles

_____ (groom) and _____ (bride),
you have decided to participate in the lighting of
candles. Our philosophy about the lighting of
these candles is perhaps unique among wedding ceremonies. On many occasions the two
outer candles have been lit, representing the
groom on your right and the bride on your left.
In the past those candles have been taken, and
the middle candle has been lit as a sign of unity.
Today we have chosen to allow the middle can-

dle to be lit from the very beginning. This represents God and His abundant love for all of us. And, as is true of every believer, we take our light from God, whose light and love are forever undiminished. From Him we receive light, and as I have already stated, we are to let our lights shine in the world for God and for His kingdom. The Bible says, "The love of God is shed abroad in our hearts by the Holy Spirit" (Rom. 5:5). As you light your separate candles, you are giving testimony of the fact that you have received from God's love, and it is this love that you are committed to let permeate your hearts and your home. I invite you to participate in the lighting of the candles.

The Pronouncement

Now, for as much as _____ (groom) and _____ (bride) have consented together in holy wedlock and have witnessed the same before God and this company, and since they have pledged their vows each to the other and have declared the same by giving and receiving rings and by joining hands, I pronounce that they are husband and wife in the name of the Father, and the Son, and the Holy Spirit. Amen. "What therefore God hath joined together, let not man put asunder" (Mark 10:9).

The groom may kiss the bride.
(The bride and groom turn to face the guests.)
Now I present to you Mr. and Mrs.
_____ (groom's full name).

Gerald Harris, Pastor
Peachtree Corners Baptist Church
Norcross, Georgia

Ceremony 11

Processional

Statement of Marriage

A wedding is obviously not the occasion for a long and detailed sermon. All the excitement of this moment itself makes me quite sure that if you are to remember anything at all now, it will have to be the simplest thing! So let me give you a text, one that sums up in itself all that I really want to say to you. It is Leviticus 6:13, and this is how it reads: "The fire shall ever be burning upon the altar; it shall never go out." And I merely want to point out three truths about it.

It Describes a Practice

This passage, Leviticus 6:8-14, describes the law of the burnt offering given by the Lord to Moses and the people of God. It also refers to part of the worship of God's people in Old Testament times, the bringing of sacrifices and offerings to the Lord and the presenting of them upon the altar as the expression of their repentance, love, and devotion to Him—the figure which, as Hebrews 9:9-15 tells us, the Lord Jesus came to fulfill as He offered Himself without spot to God (v. 14).

So upon this special altar at which the people worshiped and consecrated themselves to God, a flame burned night and day. The fire shall ever be burning upon the altar; it shall never go out (Lev. 6:13). So the first idea about this verse is that, as a historical fact, *it describes a practice,* but much more is important for us at this point.

It Suggests a Picture

For instance, how that steadily burning flame, never going out, expresses our longing for love that burns between your two hearts today! Without becoming too sentimental, it is nevertheless true that the love of your hearts burns brightly together. And this verse applied in this manner expresses our longing for your love toward each other. But even more! It expresses our longing for your love for the Lord. Charles Wesley, in one of his greatest hymns, put it like this: "Kindle a flame of sacred love, on the mean altar of thine heart. There let it for God's glory burn, with inextinguishable blaze."

Now, we rejoice that this is a Christian marriage today, and that individually the miracle of new birth has happened in your hearts; but now as you seek to bring all the future to God, your hearts—your lives and your home—let this be true: the flame shall ever be burning upon the altar. There let it for God's glory burn, with inextinguishable blaze! And that brings me to the third thought about this verse.

It Reveals a Principle

The flame did not burn untended and uncared for; it had to be cared for and fed. The passage tells us how. Each day (v. 11) the old ashes had to be cleared away. Each day (v. 12), new fuel had to be added to it, and only as that was done could the offering rise to God every day. The flame had to be tended; it was not by accident that it burned.

So it will be with your marriage. Take time to tend the flame. Do not let business commitments and ambitions or anything else cause you to neglect each other. Remove the ashes each day; never let the sun go down upon your anger. Renew the flame with something every day. How many marriages have grown utterly cold because the couple did not take the time to tend the flame!

And so it will be with your love to God. Take time to tend the flame there—every day! How busy we can become. The flame of love for God can be so easily neglected, and the Lord's Day can become the lazy day, or a day to go chasing all over the countryside, relaxing and seeing friends.

Tend the flame! God will not let the flame die, but you can neglect it 'till it becomes only a travesty of what it ought to be. Thank God, His love for us, for you, and for me has never died! It is steadfast love, love that went all the way to Calvary, love to the loveless shown that they might lovely be! And, thank God, He does not quench the smoking flax (Matt. 12:20). But let us make absolutely sure that from our side it is tended. Tend the flame! Let Charles Wesley's words be your prayer, for today and for every day:

> Jesus, confirm my heart's desire
> To work and speak and think for Thee;
> Still let me guard the holy fire,
> And still stir up Thy gift in me.

After prayer, counsel, and meditation you have reached this decisive crossroad in your life. Because you believe it is God's will for you to be one in Christ, to serve Him together in your home and through His church, and to demonstrate His love through your union, it is my privilege to ask, Who gives this woman to be married to this man?

Response: Her mother and I.

(Minister then asks couple to join hands and repeat their vows, the man being first).

Vows

I, _____ (groom), take thee _____ (bride), to be my wife in Christian marriage. I promise God, and I promise you that I will be Christian in my actions and attitudes. I will serve the Lord with you; I will provide Christian leadership in our home. I will work to meet our financial responsibilities; I will be faithful to you and to you alone. I will weep with you in sorrow, rejoice with you in blessings, and be your faithful companion until Christ calls us home. I make this vow to you, so help me God.

I, _____ (bride), take thee _____ (groom), to be my husband in the Lord. I promise God, and I promise you that I will cherish you, I will obey you, I will love you, I will provide a shoulder to cry on, a heart that understands, a warm home for you to live in, and open arms for you to lean on. I will pray for you and encourage you; I will weep when you weep, laugh when you laugh, and be yours and yours alone until our Lord separates us by death. This I solemnly and joyfully promise, so help me God.

Exchange of Rings

To portray the exchanging of your marriage vows and as a public witness of them, you will now give these beautiful rings, symbolic of your promises.

_____ (groom), repeat after me and to _____ (bride): This ring is a picture of my love for you; I give it to you to wear in joy. I give it in humble gratitude that Christ led us together. In the name of the Father, the Son, and the Holy Spirit. Amen.

_____ (bride), repeat after me and to _____ (groom). This ring is a picture of my love for you; I give it to you to wear with joy. I give it in humble gratitude that Christ led us together. In the name of the Father, the Son, and the Holy Spirit. Amen.

Prayer

Dear Father, as our Lord God Almighty, we ask You to send Your light and truth upon _____ (groom) and _____ (bride) all the days of their lives. Lord, by Your hand protect them. Father, with Your eye guide them. If it be Thy will, bestow upon them the gift and heritage of children and help them to see them brought up in the ways of the Lord. May You be glorified through this new home. In Jesus' name, Amen.

Pronouncement

Forasmuch as you, _____ (bride), and you, _____ (groom), have pledged your vows and exchanged rings symbolic of your life-long commitments to a Christian marriage and home, you have promised to encourage each other in a spiritual walk, and to assist each other in being all that Christ wants you to be, it is my happy privilege to pronounce that from this day forward, you are now husband and wife. I am happy to introduce you to Mr. and Mrs. _____ (groom's full name). (Couple may kiss; bride receives her flowers.)

> Jim Henry, Pastor
> First Baptist Church
> Orlando, Florida

Jim Henry, *The Pastor's Wedding Manual* (Nashville: Broadman Press, 1985), 155-158, 146-147, 160-161. Used by permission.

Ceremony 12

Processional

Introduction

Dearly beloved, we are assembled here in the presence of God, to join this man and this woman in holy marriage, which is instituted of God, regulated by His commandments, blessed by our Lord Jesus Christ, and to be held in honor among all persons. Let us therefore reverently remember that God has established and sanctified marriage for the welfare and happiness of mankind.

Our Savior has declared that a man shall leave his father and mother and cleave unto his wife. By His apostles He has instructed those who enter into this relationship to cherish a mutual esteem and love; to bear with each other's infirmities and weaknesses; to comfort each other in sickness, trouble, and sorrow; in honesty and industry to provide for each other, and for their household, in temporal things; to pray for and encourage each other in the concerns which pertain to God; and to live together as the heirs of the grace of life.

Forasmuch as these two persons have come hither to be made one in this holy estate, if there be any here present who know any just cause why they may not lawfully be joined in marriage, I require him now to make it known, or ever after to hold his peace.

I charge you both, before the great God, the Searcher of all hearts, that if either of you know any reason why ye may not lawfully be joined together in marriage, ye do now confess it. For be ye well assured that if any persons are joined together otherwise than as God's Word allows, their union is not blessed by Him.

Prayer

Almighty and ever-blessed God, whose presence is the happiness of every condition, and whose favor hallows every relation: We beseech Thee to be present and favorable unto these Thy servants, that they may be truly joined in the honorable estate of marriage, in the covenant of their God. As Thou hast brought them together by Thy providence, sanctify them by Thy Spirit, giving them a new frame of heart fit for their new estate; and enrich them with all grace, whereby they may enjoy the comforts, undergo the cares, endure the trials, and perform the duties of life together as becometh Christians, under Thy heavenly guidance and protection; through our Lord Jesus Christ. Amen.

Vows

_____ (Groom), wilt thou have this woman to be thy wife, and wilt thou pledge thy troth to her, in all love and honor, in all duty and service, in all faith and tenderness, to live with her, and cherish her, according to the ordinance of God, in the holy bond of marriage?

Response: I will.

_____ (Bride), wilt thou have this man to be thy husband, and wilt thou pledge thy troth to him, in all love and honor, in all duty and service, in all faith and tenderness, to live with him and cherish him, according to the ordinance of God, in the holy bond of marriage?

Response: I will.

Who giveth this woman to be married to this man?

Response: Her mother and I.

I, _____ (groom), take thee, _____ (bride), to be my wedded wife, and I do promise and covenant, before God and these witnesses, to be thy loving and faithful husband, in plenty and in want, in joy and in sorrow, in sickness and in health, as long as we both shall live.

I, _____ (bride), take thee, _____ (groom), to be my wedded husband, and I do promise and covenant, before God and these witnesses, to be thy loving and faithful wife, in plenty and in want, in joy and in sorrow, in sickness and in health, as long as we both shall live.

Rings

The groom shall say: With this ring I give thee; in token and pledge; of our constant faith; and abiding love . . .

or:

With this ring I thee wed, in the name of the Father, and of the Son, and of the Holy Spirit. Amen.

Minister may then say: Bless, O Lord, this ring, that he who gives it and she who wears it may abide in Thy peace, and continue in Thy favor, unto their life's end; through Jesus Christ our Lord. Amen.

(If a second ring is provided, a similar order shall be followed, the woman saying the same words after the minister).

Prayer

Most merciful and gracious God, of whom the whole family in heaven and earth is named: bestow upon these Thy servants the seal of Thine approval, and Thy Fatherly benediction;

granting unto them grace to fulfill, with pure and steadfast affection, the vow and covenant between them made. Guide them together, we beseech Thee, in the way of righteousness and peace, that, loving and serving Thee, with one heart and mind, all the days of their lives may be abundantly enriched with the tokens of Thine everlasting favor, in Jesus Christ our Lord. Amen.

Lord's Prayer

Pronouncement

By the authority committed unto me as a minister of the gospel, I declare that _____ (groom) and _____ (bride) are now husband and wife, according to the ordinance of God, and the law of the State—in the name of the Father, and of the Son, and of the Holy Spirit. Amen. "Whom therefore God hath joined together, let not man put asunder" (Mark 10:9).

Benediction

"The Lord bless you and keep you. The Lord make His face to shine upon you and be gracious unto you: the Lord lift up His countenance upon you, and give you peace: both now and in the life everlasting" (Num. 6:24-26). Amen.

or

God the Father, God the Son, and God the Holy Spirit, bless, preserve, and keep you; the Lord mercifully with His favor look upon you, and fill you with all spiritual benediction and grace, that ye may so live together in this life that in the world to come ye may have life everlasting. Amen.

Recessional

> Clark G. Hutchinson, Pastor
> Eastside Baptist Church
> Marietta, Georgia

Ceremony 13

Processional

Introduction

The first, the greatest, and the most sacred institution known to man is that of the home. In the sovereignty and wisdom of God it was the home, not the state or the school or even the church that was first created and divinely intended to become the cornerstone of all of life.

Whenever a man and a woman express the desire to become one, it is with the understanding that God has brought the two of them together and that they are thus to build a home under God and for God. This couple is expressing to you by their presence that they fully believe it is in the sovereign will of God that the two of them become one. So they are here this day to take their vows, not simply before you but primarily before God. The vows they make will mainly be to God and only then to each other.

The Bible teaches that marriage is to be a permanent relationship of one man and one woman totally committed to the Lord Jesus Christ and totally committed to each other. Therefore, let it be said what God has joined together, let no man put asunder (Mark 10:9).

Dear friends, we have assembled here in the presence of God to unite this couple in marriage and to seal the sacred rights of matrimony. Who gives this woman to this man in wedlock?

Response of bride's parents: We do.

The two cornerstones of a successful marriage are love and commitment. The Bible gives a crystal-clear definition of the only kind of love that will last through the winds of adversity which will surely blow through any marriage. Paul speaks of that love in 1 Corinthians 13:

> Love is patient, love is kind, and is not jealous. Love does not brag and is not arrogant. It does not act unbecomingly; it does not seek its own, is not provoked, does not take into account a wrong suffered, does not rejoice in unrighteousness, but rejoices with the truth; bears all things, believes all things, hopes all things, endures all things (1 Cor. 13:4-7, NASB).

It must be understood that the kind of love of which the Bible speaks is not a sentimental emotion that can pass away with time, but it is a commitment of the will that lasts for all eternity.

The second cornerstone is that of commitment. There must be the commitment of the husband to love his wife in a godly manner and to lead his home spiritually. Likewise there must be the commitment of the wife to submit to her husband's leadership and to respond to his love with her own respect and love. The Bible describes the husband-wife relationship in this way:

> Wives be subject to your own husbands as to the Lord for the husband is the head of the wife as Christ also is the Head of the church, He himself being the Savior of the body. But as the church is subject to Christ so also the wives ought to be to their husbands in everything. Husbands love your wives just as Christ also loved the church and gave himself up for her that he might sanctify her, having cleansed her by the washing of water with the Word of God. So husbands ought also to love their own wives as their own bodies. He who loves his own wife loves himself (Eph. 5:22-26, NASB).

So to this couple I say: If you are willing to commit yourself to the sacredness and the sanctity of the holy covenant you are about to make with each other, and if you know of no barrier to such a union between yourselves, you will signify such by joining your hands together.

Prayer

Vows

Do you, _____ (groom), in the presence of God and these assembled witnesses, promise to love and to cherish in sickness and in health, in prosperity and in adversity, this woman whose right hand you now hold? Do you promise to be to her in all things a true and faithful husband, to cleave unto her and to her only as long as life shall last? Do you?

Response: I do.

Do you take her to be your lawfully wedded wife as long as you both shall live? Do you commit yourself to her happiness and her self-fulfillment as a Christian and to her usefulness in the kingdom of God? Do you?

Response: I do.

Do you, _____ (bride), in the presence of God and these assembled witnesses, promise to love and to cherish in sickness and in health, in prosperity and in adversity, this man whose right hand you now hold? Do you promise to be to him in all things a true and faithful wife, to cleave unto him and to him only as long as life shall last?

Do you?

Response: I do.

Do you take him to be your lawfully wedded husband as long as you both shall live? Do you commit yourself to his happiness and his self-fulfillment as a Christian and to his usefulness in the kingdom of God?

Do you?

Response: I do.

Do you possess a token of your love and affection to give to your bride as a seal of this holy covenant? Do you?

Response: I do.

What is it?

Response: A ring.

This ring is more than an ornament or a piece of jewelry. It is the symbol of absolute and total commitment of one person to another in marital love. It has no ending, symbolizing the unending love and commitment which you vow to have for this woman, even unto death. It is also symbolic of a sacred vow that you have taken, not only before mankind, but primarily before God. This ring is both a sign and a seal of your sacred vow and is to be a ceaseless reminder of the sacred commitment you are making to this woman. Place the ring on the wedding finger of your bride and repeat after me.

I _____ (groom), take thee, _____ (bride), to be my wedded wife. I take thee for richer for poorer, for better for worse, in sickness and in health, as long as we both shall live. I pledge to be the spiritual leader in our home and submit myself and my family totally to the lordship of Jesus Christ. I make this vow in the name of the Father, and of the Son, and of the Holy Spirit. Amen.

_____ (Bride), do you possess a token of our love and affection to give to your husband as a seal of this holy covenant? Do you?

Response: I do.

What is it?

Response: A ring.

The ring you have received represents an eternal commitment on the part of your husband to love you always. The ring you are about to give carries with it the same commitment. This ring is to be a ceaseless reminder to you that your love for your husband is to be second only to the love you have for your Lord and Savior, Jesus Christ. Place this ring on the wedding finger of your husband and repeat after me.

I, _____ (bride), take thee, _____ (groom), to be my wedded husband. I take thee for richer for poorer, for better for worse, in sickness and in health, as long as we both shall live. With this ring I vow to submit to your spiritual leadership and to live a life of holiness, purity, and honor. I pledge to be your helpmate in building a home under the lordship of Jesus Christ. I make this vow in the name of the Father, and of the Son, and of the Holy Spirit. Amen.

(At this point there could be a prayer, a song, and a lighting of a unity candle.)

Unity Candle

The bride and groom will now light the unity candle, signifying that they are no longer two, but they are one in the Lord Jesus Christ, having left father and mother to establish their own family under God.

Pronouncement

Now by virtue of the authority invested in me as a minister of Jesus Christ our Lord, in the presence of God and these assembled witnesses, I pronounce you husband and wife.

You have given sacred vows to each other before a holy and righteous God. These vows are therefore never to be broken. "What God has joined together, let not man put asunder" (Mark 10:9). You may now kiss the bride.

Ladies and gentlemen, I now present to you Mr. and Mrs. _____ (groom's full name).

Recessional

James Merritt, Pastor
First Baptist Church
Snellville, Georgia

Ceremony 14

Processional

Introduction

We come here in the name of the Lord Jesus Christ. We are here to worship and to exalt "the name that is above every name," the name of Jesus. And we are here to unite in holy matrimony _____ (groom) and _____ (bride).

Who is it that comes at this sacred moment in the lives of these two to give this woman to be the wife of this man?

Response: Her mother and I.

Prayer

Our Heavenly Father, we are thankful that when the time came for _____ (groom) to need a wife, you brought into his life _____ (bride). And when the time came for her to need a husband, you brought _____ (groom) to her.

Father, our hearts swell with thanksgiving for

the homes from which these two come, for all the training that has been poured into their lives, for parents who love and honor God as well as their children, and for parents who love each other. It is our prayer that You would accept the offering of music, the spoken word, and the gratitude of every heart as praise to You. May that which begins now continue until You separate this marriage by death or until that day when You split the heavens with a shout and come to rapture your bride, the church.

And now, Father, may every Christian feel the presence of your Spirit and may those who know not Jesus begin to put their faith and trust in Him, in whose name we pray. Amen.

_____ (groom) and _____ (bride), if God lets you live to be a hundred years of age, this will be one of the high hours of your life. This moment comes preceded by hours of prayer. From the time each one of you was born, your parents began to commit you to God. As you were raised in the church and among Christian relatives and friends, oftentimes they prayed for you that God would direct your path.

They prayed that in God's timing He would lead you each to the person who would complete you as your husband or wife. The Bible tells us that God created man. _____

(groom), He knew that it was not good, not best, for man to live alone. In His creative process He made for man that which would complete him, a woman.

Out of his side God took a rib and made a person to stand along beside him, not to be ruled by him or to rule over him, but to complete him. Where God is, love is. You remember how it was when you were a little child and you learned the Scripture, "God is love." Leave God out, and you have left love out, and what the world offers is a very poor counterfeit. But God saw that the world was drifting without purpose. Lust had been substituted for love. Man had no purpose for being here. Then Jesus came. He went to Calvary's hill and there He died. He died for our sins and He died that we "might have life and that we might have it more abundantly" (see John 10:10).

Our Lord went about doing many wonderful things when He was on earth. The first time He performed a miracle, Jesus was at a wedding. He turned the water into wine. Our Lord has never touched anything that has not been changed simply by the touch of His hand.

As you stand here, it is important to remember that both of you believe you are standing in the center of God's will. Each of you is God's person, this is God's place, this is God's time, and as you begin your life together, all that has been in your past is going to help you and give you strength, guidance, and wisdom in the years to come.

_____ (groom), when the time comes in your life that you don't know exactly how to treat your bride, simply remember how Christ treated His bride, the church, and gave Himself for her. Jesus was willing to die that the church might have life abundant and everlasting. Then, _____ (bride), when it is difficult for you to know how to respond to your husband's love in his place of leadership, just remember that the church is always in submission to the Lord. Knowing that _____ (groom) is in submission to God will make it easy for you to listen to his guidance, to encourage him, and to stand by him. Where he is weak, you will be strong, and where you are weak, you can pray that God will make him strong.

As you walk through life together, marriage will not be fifty-fifty as the world suggests; rather it will be a hundred percent on the part of each of you. _____ (groom), you are saying to _____ (bride), I plan to spend the rest of my life making you happy. And _____ (bride), you are saying to _____ (groom), I plan to spend the rest of my life making you happy.

Of all the privileges, joys, and blessings which come to a pastor, this is one of the most treasured. It is a blessed event when two people, from loving homes, having been taught the Word of God all their lives, and having had examples around them of what it is like to walk with Jesus, decide to be married. For two such persons to come together with the conviction that they can glorify our Lord more as one than as two, is a wonderful witness for all who know you now and for those who shall know you through the years.

Vows

Now, _____ (groom), I want you to repeat these vows after me to the one you have chosen to be your life's companion, I, _____ (groom), take thee, _____ (bride), to be my wedded wife, to have and hold from this day forward, for better or for worse, in riches or in poverty, in health or in sickness, in life's joys or in life's disappointments, until God in His wisdom shall separate us by death.

_____ (bride), I am going to ask you to repeat these same vows, for this is a mutual submission of each to the other, and both to the Lord. I, _____ (bride), take thee _____ (groom), to be my lawful wedded husband, to have and to hold from this day forward, for better or for worse, in riches or in poverty, in health or in sickness, in life's joys or in life's disappointments, until God in His wisdom shall separate us by death.

Exchange of Rings

_____ (groom) and _____ (bride), as I hold in my hand these beautiful wedding bands, I want you to glance at them for a moment, then I want you to look at the beautiful baptistry behind me. I want you to recall that moment in your life when you gave your heart to Jesus. You wanted to be obedient to the Lord in every area of your life. Therefore, you were baptized, picturing the death, burial, and resurrection of Jesus. When you stepped into the baptistry, you boldly took your place in obedience to the Lord and symbolically you portrayed the marvelous transaction which had happened in your life. You had died to an old life of sin, and Jesus had come to reign in your life. It was a symbol. Likewise, these rings are symbols.

You will notice that one of them is quite a bit larger than the other, and that says something about the marriage relationship. _____ (groom), you are going to be the provider and protector of your wife. You are to protect her not only from things about her on this earth but from the evil one himself. You are to pray for her daily and lift her up in the name of Jesus.

The smaller ring will be a reminder to you, _____ (bride), to pray daily that God will give _____ (groom) direction that he might be all God wants him to be and that you might be all God wants you to be. These rings are made in a complete circle. That unending circle should remind you that the Lord wants this relationship to be divided, not by a judge but only by the Judge of all judges, the King of all kings, the Lord Jesus Christ.

Would you take the smaller ring, _____ (groom), and place it on the finger of the one whom you have chosen to be your life's companion? And now, _____ (bride), would you take the other ring, and place it on the finger of the man whom you have chosen to be your life's companion?

Pronouncement

In a moment I will ask you both to kneel. First, I want you to listen to the words which you have longed to hear. As a minister of God, by the authority invested in me by the laws of this state, and by the authority which comes from God, it is my privilege to pronounce you husband and wife, and to remind you that

God's Word says what He has joined together, let no man put asunder (See Mark 10:9).

Prayer

Our Father, in the name of Jesus, we dedicate this new home to Thee. Amen.

Now you may seal the vows with a kiss. It is now my privilege for the first time to formally introduce you to Mr. and Mrs. _____ (groom's full name).

Recessional

John D. Morgan, Pastor
Sagemont Baptist Church
Houston, Texas

Ceremony 15

Processional

Introduction

_____ (groom) and _____ (bride), you honor us today by allowing us the privilege to share in this most important time in your life. We join with you joyfully and prayerfully as you exchange your vows with each other.

God's Word gives tremendous support and encouragement to marriage and the home. In the very first Book of the Bible, Genesis, God Himself designed marriage for the good of both man and woman. It is obvious from His participation at the marriage feast in Cana of Galilee that Jesus also supported the marriage contract.

The apostle Paul in the Book of Ephesians, chapter 5, develops for us a beautiful picture of the relationship in the home. We can draw from the context of that passage several charges that will be helpful to you as you make a life together.

First, I charge you to make God the center of your marriage. Paul, in Ephesians 5:18 says, "Be ye filled with the Spirit." This is your birthright as a Christian couple, so take time daily to refresh your personal lives and your marriage relationship at the well of God's Spirit. *Second, I charge you to develop an attitude of Christian joy in your relationship.* In verse 19 Paul charges, "Singing and making melody in your hearts to the Lord." The joyful attitude will be a lasting buffer between you and the evils of this world that will assail your marriage. *Third, I charge you to be mutually respectful of each other.* Paul again in verse 21 admonishes us to be subject to each other in the fear of Christ. If you develop mutual respect for each other, you will be for each other able counselors.

Marriage is sacred and holy and will require your very best. May it be so in the days ahead.

Affirmation

Will you, _____ (bride), receive _____ (groom) to be your husband? Will you promise to love him and be faithful to him until you are parted by death?

Response: I will.

_____ (groom), will you receive _____ (bride) to be your wife? Will you promise to love her and be faithful to her until you are parted by death?

Response: I will.

Presentation

Who gives _____ (bride) to be married to _____ (groom)?

Response (Usually father of the bride): Her mother and I.

There is a tender story in the Scriptures concerning a young woman by the name of Ruth. Her husband had died, leaving her a widow. At great personal sacrifice she chose to accompany her mother-in-law, Naomi, home to Bethlehem where she would be a stranger among people with strange customs. Her mother-in-law encouraged her to stay in her own land. Ruth's response has lived through the years as a classic example of the faithfulness that a husband is to demonstrate to his wife and a wife is to demonstrate to her husband. It is found in the Book of Ruth (1:16-17). And Ruth said, "Intreat me not to leave thee or to return from following after thee: for whither thou goest, I will go; and where thou lodgest, I will lodge: thy people shall be my people, and thy God my God: Where thou diest, will I die, and there will I be buried: the Lord do so to me, and more also, if aught but death part thee and me."

Let us pray.

Pastoral Prayer

Father, who gives us all of our precious and wonderful gifts, thank you for the gift of marriage. I thank you today for _____ (groom) and _____ (bride) and for the love relationship that has developed between them. It is my prayer that their relationship will grow and mature with each passing day, that the home they will establish today will be one of spiritual strength and steadfast obedience to your perfect will in their lives. We pray in their behalf for the power of the Holy Spirit in the nurturing of their relationship. In Jesus' name. Amen.

Vows

I _____ (groom), receive you, _____ (bride), to be my wife. I promise to love you in all of life's circumstances, whether in sickness or in health, whether in poverty or in wealth. I promise to love you with a love that if faithful and true until death separates us in this life.

I, _____ (bride), receive you, _____ (groom), to be my husband. I promise to love you in all life's circumstances, whether in sickness or in health, whether in poverty or in wealth. I promise to love you with a love that is faithful and true until death separates us in this life.

Ring Exchange

You have determined that you would seal your vows today by the exchanging of rings. The rings are a marvelous symbol of the vows which you have taken, and each time you touch this ring, it is my prayer that you will be reminded of the sacredness of your vows. Notice that the ring is made of gold, a symbol of purity. Your thoughts toward each other should always be pure and holy. Then notice that the ring is an unbroken circle. Your marriage is to be unbroken this side of eternity.

_____ (groom), would you place the ring on _____ (bride's) finger and share with her the pledge that this ring represents?

Groom: With this ring I pledge my love and promise to nurture that love each day of our lives.

_____ (bride), would you place the ring on _____ (groom's) finger and share with him the pledge that this ring represents.

Bride: With this ring I pledge my love and promise to nurture that love each day of our lives.

Pronouncement

On the basis of your mutual consent and my call of God to ministry, I pronounce that you are husband and wife. You have spoken your vows today. You have sealed them with the exchange of the ring which will long remind you of the seriousness of the vows you have taken. (Couple kneels at the kneeling bench.)

Pastoral Prayer

Precious Father, we seal this union today in prayer. We present this couple to You in humble submission to your divine will that their marriage will produce a witness that others might see Jesus and find newness of life in Him. In Jesus' name. Amen. You may now kiss the bride.

Following their kiss the pastor presents them Mr. & Mrs. _____ (groom's full name).

Recessional

Charles D. Page, Pastor
First Baptist Church
Charlotte, North Carolina

Ceremony 16

Processional

Introduction

_____ (groom's full name),
_____ (bride's full name), by the
grace of God you have been drawn here to this
spot in a moment that is both sacred and serious. It is serious, _____ (bride), because the
two of you come prepared to give yourselves
away. It's sacred, _____ (groom), because
you are doing so asking God's blessings upon
the very act itself. Therefore, I would like your
friends who are gathered to share with me in a
time of prayer. Would you do so please?

Prayer

Dear Heavenly Father, I thank You, Lord
God, for the homes from which these two
come. I thank You that now they propose to join
You in the creation of a new family—to join the

larger family of mankind and therein to serve You. Therefore, I do ask You to bless them at this time and their united life resulting. In Christ's name, Amen.

As there are two Testaments, the Old and the New, bound as one volume making one Book, so there are two lives that before today have been separate, but by the grace of God, they meet here to merge. May I ask, therefore, who brings this woman to be joined in holy matrimony?

Response: Her mother and I.

_____ (Groom) and _____ (bride), you two can come to this moment with confidence, knowing that the Lord Himself has profound pleasure in His children doing His will. Our beloved Christ honored a ceremony similar to this by His presence at the wedding in Cana of Galilee.

The Lord God Jehovah created the heavens and the earth and He said, "It is good." He divided the land from the sea and He said, "It is good." He separated the light from the darkness and summarily He said, "It is good." He created the birds of the air, the fish of the sea, and the animals of the earth, and He spoke, "It is good." But then, _____ (groom), He made man and He said, "It is not good that man should be alone. I will make for him an help-mate."

_____ (bride), that ancient Hebrew expression, helpmate, literally means "a second self." That in part is what the Bible speaks about when it says "two become one." You become so absorbed in each other's aspirations, ambitions, ideals, and spiritual interest so that in giving yourselves one to the other there is a kinship in Christ.

In that garden, our beloved Lord made woman, not from man's head to rule over him, not from his feet to be trodden beneath him, but from his side to be equal with him, from close to his heart to be loved by him. I take immense pleasure in sharing with you from God's Word this passage of love. I pray it will typify your life together:

> Love is patient and kind. Love does not envy. Love has no loud words in her mouth, no swelling thoughts in her heart. It is not rude or self-seeking, nor easily angry. Love finds no pleasure in evil done to others, but delights in goodness. Love knows no limit to endurance, no end of its trust, no fading of its hope. It can outlast anything. For love never fails.

Vows

Against that backdrop I'd like to ask you, _____ (groom), if you would kindly give an attentive ear to the vow portions as I state them and if each one does bespeak of your great love for _____ (bride), would you kindly repeat after me?

I, _____ (groom), take thee _____ (bride) to be my wedded wife, to have and to hold, from this day forward, in sickness or health, poverty or wealth, and to be true to you exclusively, above all else on earth, according to God's holy plan.

_____ (groom), may you have the joy that comes from complete compliance with such a complete commitment as you have just been privileged to make.

_____ (bride), if you would kindly also give an attentive ear and responsive voice if this is a summary of your love for your beloved.

I, _____ (bride), take thee _____ (groom) to be my wedded husband, to have and to hold, from this day forward, in sickness or health, poverty or wealth, and to be true to you exclusively, above all else on earth, according to God's holy plan.

May that holy plan carry the two of you ever

deeper into the depthless regions of God's un-
inhibited love, allowing you in the maturity of
your love to be more expressive of the love
which you have acknowledged here today.

Rings

In addition to the verbal exchange between
the two of you, it is appropriate that a gift
should be exchanged. The ring is fittingly used
for such a purpose. Being circular in shape,
having no end, it is thus emblematic of the enduring and unending love you have for each
other. _____ (groom), I would like to ask
you to please repeat after me. With this ring, I
thee wed, in the name of the Father, and of the
Son, and of the Holy Spirit. _____ (groom),
do you give this ring to _____ (bride) as an
evidence of your love for her?

Response: I do.

_____ (bride), will you wear this ring as a
reminder of the love that is here acknowledged
to be yours exclusively?

Response: I will.

May you have many occasions when you
pause with dignity and pride to reflect, not only
upon the beauty of the golden circle itself, but to
be reminded by it of the love that is pledged to
be yours.

This ring made of gold, a metal which is

highly resistant to tarnish, is thus pictorial of the purity of purpose that you pledge in these moments. May I ask you, therefore, _____ (bride), to repeat after me? With this ring, I thee wed, in the name of the Father, and of the Son, and of the Holy Spirit.

_____ (bride), do you give this ring to _____ (groom) as an evidence of your love for him?

Response: I do.

_____ (groom), will you in turn wear it as a token of the love that is here pledged to be yours?

Response: I will.

The two of you doubtless will on occasion be separated from each other by time and/or distance. Those rings are going to be present with you always. May they, therefore, serve as a subtle, simple, but most significant reminder of the reality that the love which you two have for each other is indeed ever present with you.

I'd like to ask one further privilege on behalf of your many guests here assembled, and that is an opportunity to pray on your behalf once more. May I ask the two of you, if you would be so gracious, as to kneel at this time to accord such a setting? May I ask each of you guests, if you would be so thoughtful, as to call the name of _____ (groom) and the name of

_____ (bride) in the ear of our Heavenly Father as we pray.

Prayer

Dear Heavenly Father, these two are here now on their knees before You as an indication of the contrition of their spirits and the commitment of themselves to you in marriage. Father, I am not going to pray in the role of folly and ask You to exempt them from problems and make them immune from difficulties, because nowhere in the Bible have You promised to do that. But I do want to thank You that You promised to be with them, to guide, guard, and govern.

Father, as they have the occasion of walking along the perimeter of the valley of the shadow of death, be there with them that they will know of Your presence and rejoice. And, oh Lord, as they walk hand in hand through the broad, sunlit uplands of victory, achievement, accomplishment, and success together, be there with them that they may know of Your presence and rejoice. For this I ask in Christ's name. Amen.

Pronouncement

_____ (Groom) and _____ (bride), being assured that there is no legal, moral, or Christian hindrance to this proper union, acting by the authority vested in me by the laws of the sovereign state of _____, as a minister of the gospel, and looking to heaven above for divine sanction, in the presence of God and these assembled witnesses, I delight to pronounce you husband and wife. Therefore, let all persons present this day take care in the sight of Jehovah God that this holy union shall ever remain sacred.

You may salute the bride (altar kiss).

Unity Candle

The couple may then move to the triple candle stand to light the unity candle as the following is read: The scripture says, "For this cause shall a man leave his father and mother and shall cleave to his wife: and they twain shall be one flesh. Wherefore, they are no more twain, but one flesh. What therefore God hath joined together, let not man put asunder."

So as the two of you, Mr. and Mrs. _____ (groom's full name) turn from this altar to walk life's path together, may you turn to do so, not as two, but as one, in the grace of our God.

Recessional

Nelson L. Price, Pastor
Roswell Street Baptist Church
Marietta, Georgia

Ceremony 17

Processional

Welcome

Welcome to this service of praise and worship as we come together to witness the marriage of _____ (groom) and _____ (bride). Surely the Lord is in this place. Let us bow our heads and ask Him for His blessing on what we are about to do.

Invocation

Our Heavenly Father, we desire to acknowledge You in every step we take in life. And, Lord, this is especially true on this, the wedding day of _____ (groom) and _____ (bride). We thank you for the love that unites them and the beauty of the marriage service. We are also thankful that what we witness today is not just a ritual, but it is a wonderful celebration of the joining together of two people who know Jesus Christ as personal Lord and Savior and who have been brought together by

Him. We acknowledge that it is within your providence and within your plan, and it is wonderful in your sight. Help us to be aware of its fullest meaning. We pray that you would bless this time and bless all who share it. In the name of Jesus Christ I pray. Amen.

Statement of Marriage

The Bible teaches that marriage is God's first institution. In the quiet Garden of Eden, before the forbidden tree had yielded its fateful fruit or the tempter had touched its inhabitants, God looked upon man and determined that it was not good for him to be alone. Then in His wisdom and grace He made a partner, a helpmeet for him, and as the Scripture says, "The Lord brought her unto the man" (Gen. 2:22). God thus established the human family, even as the heavenly hosts gave sacred witness.

Marriage was originated in divine grace, and it was designed to promote human happiness. Its vows are holy in God's sight, and they will remain the foundation of home life and social order until Jesus Christ comes to institute a new order for all mankind.

Giving of the Bride

Who now gives this woman to be married? *Response:* Her mother and I.

Vows

If you then, _____ (groom), and _____ (bride), have freely and deliberately chosen each other as partners in this holy estate and know of no reason why you should not be united in marriage, please join your right hands.

_____ (groom), in taking _____ (bride) by the right hand in token of your desire to have her as your lawful, wedded wife, before God and the witnesses present, you are promising to love, honor, and cherish her; and, leaving all others, cleave to her and be to her in all things a true and faithful husband as long as you both shall live. Do you so promise?

Response: I do.

_____ (bride), in taking _____ (groom) by the right hand to be your lawful and wedded husband before God and the witnesses present, you are promising to love him, honor, and cherish him; and, leaving all others, to cleave to him and be to him a true and faithful wife so long as both of you shall life. Do you so promise?

Response: I do.

Declaration

Then you are given to each other for richer, for poorer, for better, for worse, in sickness and in health until death shall separate you.

The apostle Paul gave us a beautiful promise in 1 Corinthians 13. He said, "Love is patient, love is kind and is not jealous. Love does not brag and is not arrogant, does not act unbecomingly; it does not seek its own, is not easily provoked, does not take into account a wrong suffered, does not rejoice in unrighteousness, but rejoices with the truth (13:4-6, NASB).

He begins to sum it up by saying, "Love bears all things, love believes all things, love hopes all things, and endures all things. . . . Love never fails. . . . Now abide faith, hope, love, these three but the greatest of these is love" (13:7,8a,13, NASB).

You are present here because you love each other. This is one of the most joyous and significant days in your lives. You have had the excitement of dating, falling in love, and being engaged, and now the day you've planned for, dreamed about, and worked toward has finally arrived—your wedding day. Gathered here with you is your family, your friends, people whom you love the most. They are people who most love you, and I thank you for the opportunity as your pastor to share in the happiness and blessing of your special day.

As I talked to both of you in preparation for your marriage, I asked what things drew you to each other. _____ (groom), your bride said that it was your compassion, generosity, and the fact that you love her unconditionally that drew her to you. And _____ (bride), your groom said your warm personality and your quiet joy were traits that drew him to you. (Note: Ministers should make their own personal observations.) I pray that these characteristics, so precious to you today, will remain through the years as fresh and meaningful as they are right now. Each of you has indicated that you appreciate the Christian spirit of the other and feels that God has given you the gift of each other. This is a marvelous beginning for a steadfast relationship that will share joy, endure hardship, and carry you arm in arm down the pathway of life. It is a marvelous privilege to feel that you have found exactly the person with whom God intended for you to spend your life.

Exchange of Rings

In the spirit of this love, you will be signifying your relationship by exchanging rings. Rings are the outward, visible sign of the invisible commitment you are making to the Lord Jesus and to each other. As you exchange these rings I ask you to be aware of how they portray the ideal marriage. The circle of the rings, with no beginning and no end, represents wholeness and a sense of eternity. The gold, the purest of all nature's metals, signifies purity in your relationship.

_____ (groom), will you place this ring on the third finger of your bride's left hand and repeat these vows after me? With this ring, I thee wed; and all my worldly goods I thee endow; in the name of the Father, the Son, and the Holy Spirit.

_____ (bride), likewise, will you place this ring on the third finger of your groom's left hand and repeat these vows after me? With this ring I thee wed; and all my worldly goods I thee endow in the name of the Father, the Son, and the Holy Spirit.

Prayer of Dedication

Father, as _____ (groom) and _____ (bride) dedicate themselves to each other and to you, I pray that the love between them will grow sweeter with the passing of the years. May they always trust each other and in perfect confidence may they trust in you. Lord, I thank you for the mystery of marriage that they are going to discover. Mysteriously it cuts sorrow in half because there are two to share the burden; and it doubles the joys because there are two to share the joyous experiences. From the depths of my heart I offer petition for two things for their home: I pray that Jesus Christ will always be acknowledged as their Lord. And I pray that laughter will ring from their home each day of the year, signifying the happiness of those who dwell there. Father, I ask these blessings in Jesus' name. Amen.

Unity Candle

_____ (groom) and _____ (bride) are going to light the unity candle, symbolizing that in marriage they are no longer two people, but in Christ they become one flesh.

Pronouncement

For as much as _____ (groom) and _____ (bride) have agreed together according to the teachings of Scripture and the laws of this State, I, as a minister of the gospel, declare they are husband and wife. "What therefore God has joined together, let not man put asunder" (Mark 10:9). You may kiss your bride.

Benediction

Father, we ask your blessings on these friends as they build a life together. May it be a life of mutual respect, encouraging each other to be the best they can be for your sake. And now may the grace, mercy, and peace of God, and the fellowship of His Holy Spirit rest on them and on each of us now and forevermore. Amen.

Presentation

It is now my pleasure to be the first to present to you Mr. and Mrs. _____ (groom's full name).

Recessional

> Dwight "Ike" Reighard, Pastor
> New Hope Baptist Church
> Fayetteville, Georgia

Ceremony 18

Processional

Introduction

Dearly beloved, we are gathered together in the sight of God and these assembled witnesses to join this man and this woman in holy matrimony, which is an honorable estate instituted by God and signifying unto us the mystical union which exists between Christ and His church. It is therefore not to be entered into unadvisedly but reverently, discreetly, and in the fear of God.

Into this estate these two persons come now to be joined. As the same gracious God who gave the first wife to her husband comes now to give this woman to this man, I ask then who in behalf of our Heavenly Father gives _____ (bride) to _____ (groom)?

Response (by father, family member, or friend): I do, her mother and I, and the like.

Prayer

I charge you both as you stand in the presence of God to remember that love and loyalty alone will avail as the foundation of a happy home. If the solemn vows which you are about to make be kept inviolate, and if steadfastly you endeavor to do the will of your Heavenly Father, your life will be full of joy, and the home which you are establishing will abide in peace. No other human ties are more tender, no other vows more sacred than those you now assume.

Vows

_____ (groom), wilt thou have this woman to be thy wedded wife, to live together in the holy estate of matrimony? Wilt thou love her, honor her, and keep her in sickness and in health, and forsaking all others, keep thee unto her so long as you both shall live? If you so promise, reply I will.

Response: I will.

_____ (bride), wilt thou have this man to be thy wedded husband, to live together in the holy estate of matrimony? Wilt thou love him, comfort him, honor him, and keep him in sickness and in health, and forsaking all others, keep thee unto him so long as you both shall live? If you so promise, reply I will.

Response: I will.

_____ (groom), will you show your sincerity in these vows by taking _____ (bride) by the right hand and repeating after me? . . . I, _____ (groom), take thee _____ (bride) to be my wedded wife, to have and to hold from this day forward, for better, for worse, for richer, for poorer, in sickness and in health, to love and to cherish till death do us part, and thereto I pledge thee my faith.

Exchange of Rings

I would have you now seal your vows with an emblem of eternity and perfection. From time immemorial the ring has been used to seal important covenants. When the race was young and parliaments unknown, the great seal of state was fixed upon a ring, and its stamp was the sole sign of imperial authority. Friends often exchanged the simple band of gold as enduring evidence of good will, while many a hero and heroine of immortal song and thrilling tale tread winding paths of intrigue and adventure safe and unhurt, bearing as a magic talisman the signet of some great benefactor. From such impressive precedents the golden circlet, most prized of treasures, has come to its loftiest prestige in the symbolic significance it vouches at the matrimonial altar. Here untarnishable material and unique form become the precious tokens of the pure and abiding qualities of the ideal marital state. As the ring is never ending but complete in its form so is your marriage to be endless and complete in your love, one for another. _____ (groom), would you place this ring upon _____ (bride's) finger? _____ (groom), repeat after me, With this ring I wed thee now and with all I am and have I thee endow. _____ (bride), repeat after me: I take this pledge of thee and in return I give a wife's best love as long as God may let us live. _____ (bride), would you place this ring upon _____ (groom's) finger? Do you _____ (bride) give this ring to _____ (groom) as a token of your love for him?

Response: I will.

Will you, _____ (groom), take this ring as a token of _____ (bride's) love for you, and will you wear it as a token of your love for her?

Response: I will.

Pronouncement

For as much as _____ (groom) and _____ (bride) have consented together in holy wedlock and have witnessed the same before God and this company and hereto have given and pledged their faith each to the other and have declared the same by giving and receiving the rings and by joining hands, I pronounce that they are husband and wife in the name of the Father and the Son and the Holy Ghost. "What therefore God hath joined together, let not man put asunder" (Mark 10:9).

Now beloved, you have entered upon a new life. A new day has dawned for both. Search diligently God's blessed Word for the duties you owe to Him and to each other. To your own selves be true. This do and lo the kingdom of heaven is near you—even within your own heart.

Prayer

Recessional

>   Ralph Smith, Pastor
>   Hyde Park Baptist Church
>   Austin, Texas

Ceremony 19

Processional

Introduction

What is there in all the world which can bind two people together, to live together all the days of their lives, happily contented and satisfied? Some might say, "Mutual goals." Others might say, "The same philosophy about life." Yet the only factor that can bind two people together is love. Love is patient, kind, and envies no one. Only love will deliver a satisfying and fulfilling life all the days of your lives. Love is the only glue which God has ever given to bind two people together. Paul describes it in this fashion. "Love is never boastful, or conceited, nor rude, nor selfish, not quick to take offense, love keeps no score of wrongs, does not gloat over other men's sins, but delights in the truth. There is nothing love cannot face. No limit to its faith, its hope, and its endurance. Love will never come to an end" (See 1 Cor. 13:4-8*a*).

The reason you and I are here is because God has placed that quality of love in the hearts of _____ (groom) and _____ (bride). Having already become one in the Lord Jesus Christ, they come now to become one in marriage. They are confident that the love which God has placed in each of their hearts is of a lifetime quality. Why? Because it is God's love.

The Scripture states that God is love. When God indwells the heart of a man and He indwells the heart of a woman, and attracts the two to each other, it is His Will to make them one. Then the love He has placed in each of their hearts is more than sufficient to build into their lives everything their hearts desire. So we are here not because two people fell in love but because two people who love the Lord Jesus Christ gave themselves to Him, and in the process of that beautiful surrender, He made everything right. Thus we are here by an act of God's sovereign will.

While the romanticism of love is very important, it is always secondary to the love which God places in their hearts for each other. _____ (groom) and _____ (bride), how grateful we all are that God has brought you together, saved you for each other, and kept you through the years in order to fulfill His purpose and His plan for your lives. As you know, this is not the end of anything but the beginning of something very wonderful. When two people are made one in the Lord Jesus Christ there is the potential of fulfillment, of achievement, and of accomplishment in life that is not true when there is no such union. So I want to remind you, _____ (groom), that by taking _____ (bride) to be your wife, you are assuming the awesome, sobering, and adult responsibility of a husband. You are saying to God, to her, and to her parents, as well as to your own self, that you are willing for God to work into your life all the experiences and all the qualities that are essential in helping her to become the person whom God wants her to be. Therefore, having trusted the Lord Jesus Christ as your Savior and appropriating His life in your life, you are to depend upon the Holy Spirit to guide you and lead you day by day. While you take on a wonderful responsibility you also take on an awesome one. When God puts two people together He makes them both responsible to Him.

_____ (bride), you are to understand as _____ (groom) understands that God has put you two together for His divine purpose. You must never forget that your own pleasure and enjoyment in life ultimately depends upon the fulfillment of God's purpose in your life.

And I am sure, _____ (bride), that you understand because your obedience to God has been a beautiful testimony among us. What a joy it is for us to see God put you and _____ (groom) together. No doubt, _____ (bride), you recall your own responsibility to your husband. You are to be the kind of godly wife a Christian man needs. As God said, you are to be a helpmeet, a motivator, and one who supports her husband. Of all the women in the world whom He could have chosen, God chose you to be _____ (groom's) wife. Of all the men in the world whom He could have chosen, _____ (groom), God chose you to be _____ (bride's) husband. Therefore, you must both accept mutual responsibility to make your marriage one of lasting love.

We come now to thank God for bringing you to this point in your lives. This occasion is not the end of your dreams but simply a chapter in those dreams. And so we want to say thanks to God for His goodness, love, mercy, and grace which He has bestowed upon you. How grateful we are for your parents who taught you both about courtesy, kindness, generosity, and all the rest. God has worked in both of your lives to equip you and to prepare you for this day and for all the rest of your days together. Because this is true, I require and charge you both in the presence of God to remember that love and loyalty alone will prevail as the foundation of a happy and enduring home. No other human ties are more tender, and no other vows more sacred than those you now assume. And if these solemn vows are kept and steadfastly you endeavor to do the will of your Heavenly Father, the home you are establishing will abide in peace and love and fulfillment.

Vows

_____ (groom), I want to ask you first if you will take _____ (bride) to be your wedded wife, to live together in the holy state of matrimony? Will you love her, comfort her, honor and keep her, and forsaking all others, keep thee only unto her so long as you both shall live?

Response: I will.

_____ (bride), will you have _____ (groom) to be your wedded husband to live together in the holy state of matrimony? Will you love him, comfort him, honor and keep him, in sickness and in health, and forsaking all others, keep thee only unto him so long as you both shall live?

Response: I will.

And who giveth _____ (bride)?

Response: Her mother and I.

I _____ (groom), take thee _____ (bride) to be my wedded wife, to have and to hold, from this day forward, for better for worse, for richer for poorer, in sickness and in health, to love and to cherish till death us do part, according to God's holy law, and to you I pledge my love.

I _____ (bride), take thee _____ (groom) to be my wedded husband, to have and to hold, from this day forward, for better for worse, for richer for poorer, in sickness and in health, to love and to cherish, till death us do part, according to God's holy law, and to you I pledge my love.

Exchange of Rings

This ring is an outward and visible sign signifying the uniting of _____ (groom) and _____ (bride) in holy wedlock through the church of the Lord Jesus Christ. The ring is a token of their love each to the other. May we pray.

Our Father, as these rings are given and received I pray that the Holy Spirit will write indelibly upon their minds and their hearts the true meaning of these rings. They are untarnished, unbroken, and that is the way you intend their marriage to be all the days they may live. You have filled them with Thy Spirit to make it possible. Now as they give and as they receive each other, having pledged their love, their loyalty and their devotion, I pray that the Holy Spirit will bind them together in such a beautiful bond so as to cause them to sing your praises for giving to them each other. This I pray in Christ's name, Amen.

Groom: In token and pledge, of the vows between us made, with this ring I thee wed. In the Name of the Father, and the Son, and the Holy Spirit. Amen.

Bride: In token and pledge, of the vows between us made, with this ring I thee wed. In the Name of the Father, and the Son, and the Holy Spirit. Amen.

Pronouncement

For as much as _____ (groom) and _____ (bride) have consented together in holy wedlock and have joined hands and have given and received rings, I pronounce them husband and wife in the name of the Father, the Son, and the Holy Spirit. "Those whom God hath joined together let no man put asunder" (see Mark 10:9).

Prayer

Father, thank You for the wonderful gift of love, for there is nothing in all of the earth to compare with it. Love is the unseen, but so easily felt, method by which You bind two people together to live through the difficulties, the heartaches, the trials, and the sorrows of life. Then the joys and mountain peaks of life are indescribable, indefinable, and incomparable. We thank You that your love is sufficient and adequate for every changing experience of life. We thank You, Father, for _____ (groom) and for _____ (bride) and for Christ who lives within them. We thank You for the depth of their understanding of Christ and of His ways. Thank You for teaching them spiritual truths which have prepared them for this day and for the days ahead. We thank You for every person who has contributed to the solid and firm foundation of their lives.

They stand before us equipped to live in a way which will honor You, glorify You, and praise You. We ask in their behalf that You would grant them both wisdom beyond human understanding—divine wisdom. Grant to them discernment in decisions, and may they always be wise enough to ask the question, "Lord, what wilt Thou have us to do?" I pray that You will grant them increasing faith. May they be willing to have their faith stretched. May they be willing to grow because their ultimate goal is not merely the satisfaction of each other but the pleasing of You, their Heavenly Father.

May their marriage be a beautiful overflow of an indescribable love from above which mankind can never imitate in any form or fashion. May others see the love of Christ Jesus within them as they love each other. I pray You will help them to understand that every experience is always an opportunity to discover something new about You, as well as something new about each other. For surely as two people grow toward You they must always grow closer to each other. I pray, Father, that they will look to You as the source for every single need, for there is no reason for them ever to be in need unless You find it necessary to gain their attention. Even then may they listen in order that the need shall be supplied. I pray their marriage will be characterized in such a manner that it will become a challenge and a hope for others who are waiting for marriage. I pray that You will protect their home, that You will protect their house, and that they will always look to You as their Divine Protector and Provider. So we ask in their behalf the very best of Heaven's blessings now and in all the days to come. Father, keep ever before them the simple truth that You have put them together to glorify and to honor You.

This I pray in Jesus' name and for His sake. Amen.

Recessional

> Charles Stanley, Pastor
> First Baptist Church
> Atlanta, Georgia

Ceremony 20

Processional

Introduction

We are here for a sacred occasion, one which is sweet and special to you, to your families, and to all your friends who are here to share it with you. A perfect marriage is made in heaven. A perfect marriage is a union of three: Christ, a man, and a woman. Before the foundation of the world God ordained that the two of you would be together. He has engineered and used every circumstance in your lives up to this point to prepare the two of you to become one in Him.

I remind you this is the only relationship this side of heaven of which the Bible says that two people become one flesh. You are entering into a covenant with Jesus Christ and with all of your brothers and sisters who are in a covenant with Him, but also a marriage covenant with each other. You must remember that you are not only making vows to each other but also to the Lord Jesus as well.

We are in covenant with Jesus because He surrendered His all to God in our behalf and died our death on the cross, taking our sin, our suffering, our shame, our sorrow, our separation. Today you enter into the marriage covenant by saying you die to selfishness and to the single life. You surrender your all to the Father. You surrender your all to each other. The making of a covenant traditionally includes an exchange. When we entered into covenant with Jesus we exchanged our lives for His life, exchanging all that we are for all that He is and all that He has.

David and Jonathan enacted a covenant. In 1 Samuel 18, they entered into a covenant to be life-long friends. They exchanged their coats. They exchanged their weapons. The exchange meant that they were exchanging their friends for each other's friends; their enemies for each other's enemies; their curses; their blessings. They exchanged all those things so that, whenever you spoke of one, you definitely spoke of the other.

Today you are exchanging all that you are and all that you have with each other. It is no longer "I," "me," and "mine." From now on it shall we "we," "us," and "ours." _____ (groom), _____ (bride) is taking this exchange so seriously that she is exchanging her name for your name. After today she will no longer be known as _____ (bride's given and family name), but instead she will be known as _____ (bride's given and family name plus groom's family name), and that is a very serious matter for her to be willing to make that exchange. Furthermore, a covenant involves an examination. We are able to examine our relationship with Christ on a daily basis. Let a man examine himself for the Bible says, "Wherefore let him that thinketh he standeth take heed lest he fall" (1 Cor. 10:12).

In olden days when two people entered into a covenant, they would on occasion meet again to examine the conditions of that covenant for the purpose of making sure that both of them were remaining true to the commitment. You need to examine your covenant relationship in marriage in days to come, _____ (groom), by considering daily whether or not you are loving your wife as Christ loved the church and gave Himself for her. You must examine your heart to make sure that you are willing to die for _____ (bride) and make the sacrifices necessary to promote her safety, her security, her strength, and her welfare. God has placed in her unique characteristics that He wants you to develop and bring out in her life.

_____ (bride), daily you must examine your own heart, your own covenant relationship, and make sure that you are submitted to your own husband as unto the Lord. Daily you will need to examine your heart to make sure that you mutually submit to the Christ who indwells the two of you.

So God tells us in 1 Corinthians 7 and Ephesians 5 His exact view of marriage. _____ (groom), the Bible says it is ordained that a man should leave his father and his mother and should cleave unto his wife that the two of them should be one flesh, united in all hopes, aims, sentiments, and interests of this present time (see Mark 10:7-8). So I remind you that you are not entering into a secular experiment but into a spiritual experience because God takes this relationship so seriously that He likens it to the relationship that exists between Christ and His church, Christ being the groom, His fellowship of believers being His bride.

Vows

So, _____ (groom), if you and _____ (bride) have freely and deliberately chosen each other as partners in this holy estate, and you know of no just cause why you should not be so united, in token thereof, will you please join your right hands? _____ (groom), in taking _____ (bride), whom you hold by the right hand, to be your lawful and wedded wife, you must promise before the Lord and the witnesses present that you will love her, honor her, and cherish her in that relationship, and leaving all others, you'll cleave only unto her. You must lead her in all things at all times in all ways, a true and faithful husband as long as you both shall live. Do you make that promise to the Lord and to _____ (bride)?

Response: I do.

_____ (groom), I'd like for you to look at your bride now and repeat this vow after me to her: I, _____ (groom), take thee _____ (bride), to be my lawful wedded wife, to have and to hold, to love and to cherish, for richer or poorer, for better or worse, in sickness and in health, till death do us part.

Now, _____ (bride), you will look at _____ (groom) and repeat after me to him: I, _____ (bride), take thee _____ (groom), to be my lawful wedded husband, to have and to hold, to love and to cherish, for richer or poorer, for better or worse, in sickness and in health, till death do us part.

Exchange of Rings

You have chosen rings today as the seal and as the symbol of your wedding covenant. They are made of gold, a metal that is not easily tarnished and one that endures a long time, and I want you to remember as you place these rings on your hands today that they are a symbol of the unbroken marital union that a holy God is establishing today, and they must never be preyed upon by an outside force in any way.

_____ (groom), as a token of this hour and of the vows that you are making to the Lord and to _____ (bride), I want you to place this ring on her hand and repeat this vow after me to her: With this ring I thee wed. With loyal love I thee endow and all my worldly goods with thee I share. In the name of the Father and the Son and the Holy Ghost. Blessed be forevermore.

_____ (Groom), you gave to _____ (bride) a diamond, an engagement ring. It was the earnest, the down payment, the initial promise you were making to her that one day you were going take her to be your bride. Today you are fulfilling that promise. Therefore, I want you to take this engagement ring and slip it back on her finger over her wedding band and

I want you to tell _____ (bride) in your own words how much she means to you and why you have come at this time to fulfill the promise you made to her _____ ago. (Groom expresses his love).

_____ (bride), as a ceaseless reminder of the hour and the vows that you are making to God and to _____ (groom), I want you to place this ring on his hand, and I want you to repeat this vow after me to him: With this ring I thee wed. With loyal love I thee endow. All my worldly goods with thee I share in the name of the Father and the Son and the Holy Ghost. Blessed be forevermore.

Pronouncement

_____ (groom), _____ (bride), inasmuch as the two of you have followed the Lord's leadership freely and deliberately, you have chosen to be partners in holy matrimony in the sight, power, and strength of the Lord Jesus. Inasmuch as you have made your vows to the Lord and to each other, and have sealed these vows by the giving and receiving of rings, according to the authority of God's Word, and according to the authority vested in me by the state of _____ as an ordained minister of the gospel, I hereby pronounce you husband

and wife. What God hath joined together, let no man ever make any attempt to put asunder (see Mark 10:9). Now let the first moments of your marriage begin in prayer.

To those of you who know the Lord and exercise your throne right to pray, would you please lift a prayer for _____ (groom) and _____ (bride)? I'm going to commit them to the Lord in the opening moments of their marriage, but would you minister to them by lifting them up to the Lord and praying for them?

Prayer

_____ (groom) and _____ (bride), God bless you. We love you and pray God's richest blessings upon you. _____ (groom), you may now kiss your bride.

Unity Candle

_____ (groom) and _____ (bride), will you now light the unity candle, symbolizing two things: that Christ is your Light, and now you are no longer two separate entities but have become one identity in the Lord Jesus. He is the Light of the world. He is your Light, and you are an extension of Him, sharing that Light with the whole world.

Now, ladies and gentlemen, I have the esteemed honor and privilege as their pastor, of introducing to you officially for the first time, Mr. and Mrs. _____ (groom's name).

Recessional

> Len Turner, Pastor
> Calvary Baptist Temple
> Savannah, Georgia

Ceremony 21

Processional

Prayer

Heavenly Father, we have come to the altar of the church to link these two lives into one. We pray, our Father, that Thou will come and pour out Thy blessings on these two young people. We thank Thee, our Father, for all the glorious circumstances in their lives that have brought them to this time and place. We thank Thee in Thy good providence that You have watched over them, protected them, and brought them to this love which they now feel in their hearts.

We all pray that You will give them long lives of usefulness and happiness. We pray, our Father, that no tragedy will ever fall across their path, and if it please Thee, we pray that You will give them glorious success in their daily work, and that they will always be mindful to keep their faces turned toward Thee. We thank Thee, our Father, for the Christian heritage which is theirs. We thank Thee for the hands of the fathers and mothers who have guided them until this hour. We pray that You will help them to realize that as recipients of Christian training their lives encompass a greater responsibility. Help them to make this an altar of dedication where they will recommit themselves to all the deep Christian principles which they have learned across the years. We pray as they go out into life that You will help them increasingly to learn the lessons of unselfishness, and that they will live more and more for Thee and for others and less and less for themselves.

We pray that they will always keep their feet on the road that leads to the church when the Lord's Day comes. We pray that they will always keep the Bible open in their home so every day they can look in Thy priceless and perfect Book and receive instruction for daily living. Now, our Father, we know there is no tie we can make unless You tie them together, and we pray that it may be so now. We make our prayer in Christ's name. Amen.

Introduction

It is my privilege to remind you that marriage is a very sacred institution. Of all the institutions on this earth, there is none more sacred than the one we call marriage. As you know, marriage did not come from the hand or the mind of man but from God. When you turn to the book we call the Bible, you will read in its very first pages the story of how God created man. It says that God breathed into man the breath of life and he became a living soul (See Gen. 2:7). And the Bible says that God visited the man which He had made and God found that the man was lonely (See Gen. 2:18). With His own fingers, He reached inside the man's body, took part of it, and formed woman.

Years ago, I read that someone said He reached in and took that part of man's body nearest his heart because woman was to be loved by the man, and He took the part of the man's body that was underneath his arm because the woman was to be protected by the man. And God brought the woman He had made to the man and the record says, The man loved the woman. And God said, So shall it be from henceforth, one man loving one woman, one woman loving one man (See Gen. 2:24). That was God's first plan for marriage, and that is still God's plan today.

Then you remember when Jesus, our Lord, came down to the earth to live, and though He was never a married man, He did understand marriage. He went into the homes of the people, and He blessed their home life. On one occasion they invited Him to attend a wedding in the little town of Cana of Galilee. He not only attended the wedding, but there He performed His first miracle, showing that God's divine approval is on this institution we call marriage.

(Use this where it applies.) Both of you are not only believers, but you have sought through the years to live the Christian life. Therefore, this wedding takes on added significance.

_____ (groom), you were _____ years of age when you and your parents came to the church. Soon after, you accepted Christ and you were baptized. Later on your sisters accepted Christ and were baptized and then your brother. I watched your family grow. I remember the day you went away to the university. Soon I began to hear of your great Christian influence as a member of the football team.

_____ (groom), I remind you that you will be the one who will set the tone in your home. Keep the Bible open. Never sit down with your family to eat your daily food that you do not lift up your voice in prayer and praise to God. Also, be an example for your wife and any children that God may give you. They will follow in your steps. If your steps are right and directed toward the Lord, you will lead your own family closer to Christ. Because of your heritage, I ask you, make the spot where you are standing now a spot of dedication.

(Use such personal information only as you feel led.)_____ (bride), you have inherited a great tradition. A number of years ago your father and mother stood before me here as you do. Now here you stand. Not only are you a Christian, but you are a mature Christian woman. I have watched you mature, and for that I am grateful. Now you have come to the time when you can offer much. You have heard me say often that the greatest thing any woman can do is to teach one man what true love really is. How I trust that will be your daily task and if God does give you children, be very, very sure that you train them to walk in the way which you have known.

Therefore, this becomes a serious moment for a Christian woman who is ready now to give herself and her life to the man she loves. Make this a moment of real dedication.

Vows

As we come now to take these sacred vows, who gives this woman to be this man's bride?

Response: Her mother and I.

If you then, _____ (groom) and _____ (bride) have freely and deliberately chosen each other as partners in this holy estate, and you know no reason why you should not be so united, in token thereof, please join right hands.

_____ (groom), in taking _____ (bride), whom you hold by the right hand to be your lawful and wedded wife, before God and these witnesses present, you must promise to love her, honor and cherish her in that relationship, and leaving all others, cleave only unto her, and be to her in all things a true and faithful husband, so long as you both shall live. Do you so promise?

Response: I do.

Then will you repeat after me these vows? I, _____ (groom), take thee _____ (bride), to have and to hold, for richer or for poorer, for better or for worse, in sickness and in health, till death do us part.

_____ (bride), in taking _____ (groom) whom you hold by the right hand to be your lawful and wedded husband, before God and these witnesses present, you must promise to love him, to honor and cherish him in that relationship, and leaving all others, cleave only unto him, and be to him in all things a true and a faithful wife, so long as you both shall live. Do you so promise?

Response: I do.

Then will you repeat after me these vows? I, _____ (bride), take thee _____ (groom), to have and to hold, for richer or for poorer, for better or for worse, in sickness and in health, till death do us part.

Exchange of Rings

And now to remind you of these vows that you have just taken, there will be an exchange of rings. _____ (groom), place this ring on the hand of your bride. _____ (bride), place this ring on the hand of your groom. These little golden bands which you have just exchanged are unending to remind you every day that the tie which binds your lives together is an unending tie.

Pronouncement

Acting on the authority which is vested in me by the laws of the state of _____, and looking to heaven for God's divine approval, I now pronounce you husband and wife. Will you always remember to keep these words in your heart? "Entreat me not to leave thee or to return from following after thee, for whither thou goest, I will go, and where thou lodgest, I will lodge. Thy people shall be my people and thy God, my God. Where thou diest, will I die and there will I be buried. The Lord do so to me and more also if aught but death part me and thee" (Ruth 1:16-17).

Benediction

Will you bow your heads? And now, "may the Lord bless thee and keep thee: May the Lord lift up His countenance upon thee and give thee peace" (Num. 6:24-26). Amen.

Recessional

The late W. O. Vaught, Pastor Emeritus
Immanuel Baptist Church
Little Rock, Arkansas

Ceremony 22

Processional

Biblical Foundation for Marriage
(Father of the Groom)

The Bible says Let marriage be held in honor among all. Let the marriage bed be undefiled (See Heb. 13:4). Let every man have his own wife, and let every woman have her own husband (See 1 Cor. 7:2).

An excellent wife is the crown of her husband. Listen to God's Word.

Wives, submit yourselves unto your own husbands, as unto the Lord. For the husband is the head of the wife. Even as Christ is the head of the church: and he is the Saviour of the body. Therefore as the church is subject unto Christ, so let the wives be to their own husbands in every thing. Husbands, love your wives, even as Christ also loved the church, and gave himself for it (Eph. 5:22-25). So ought men

to love their wives as their own bodies. He
that loveth his wife loveth himself (v. 28).
For this cause shall a man leave his father
and mother, and shall be joined unto his
wife, and they two shall be one flesh (v.
31).

Let the husband render unto the wife
due benevolence: and likewise also the
wife unto the husband. The wife hath not
power of her own body, but the husband:
and likewise also the husband hath not
power of his own body, but the wife. De-
fraud ye not one the other, except it be with
consent for a time (1 Cor. 7:3-5). Wives, be
submissive to your husbands. Husbands,
likewise love your wives and live with your
wives in an understanding way as the
weaker vessel. Grant her the honor as a fellow heir of the grace of life (1 Pet. 3:7).

I've heard many women say, "If he really
loved me like Christ loved the church, then I
would submit myself to him." I've heard many
men say, "If she would submit herself to me, I
would love her like Christ loved the church."
Let me say to you that no man has ever loved
any woman like Christ loved the church. But at
the same time He is our Example, the One who
died for the church, the One who protects the

church, the One who is an advocate for every
believer in the church. Likewise, the husband is
to love his wife sacrificially. In the same spirit a
wife is to love her husband and submit herself
to him.

Men have said, "I believe marriage is a 50-
50 proposition. She doesn't come halfway."
Women have said, "He doesn't meet me halfway." I have found that the church is not a 50-50
proposition, but it's a 100-100 proposition.
When you love her enough to die for her, when
you submit to him like the church submits to
the Savior, your marriage will be most blessed.

Prayer (Given by the father of the groom)

Father of the groom then asks, Who giveth
this woman in marriage to this man?
Response: Her mother and I.

Introduction (Father of the bride)

This is a first for me today, so I've written a
special ceremony. _____ (bride) knows I am
not too formal. Nevertheless, I hope you will listen attentively and prayerfully as we share in
this special time together.

_____ (bride), you and _____
(groom) come to this holy and heaven-
sanctioned occasion with immeasurable blessings attending you. You come by God's loving

providence which has graciously led you every step of your lives. You stand here as products of Christian parents who conceived you, cared for you, and led you to know Jesus as your personal Savior. You are surrounded by friends, seen and unseen, who have prayed for you and shared your lives. You are especially blessed in that. As did those in Cana of Galilee, you have invited Jesus to attend your wedding. He has accepted your invitation and is the unseen One who lends meaning and spiritual warmth to this moment. So, thus blessed, you will now give heed to the vows you are to make to one another.

Vows

_____ (groom), the Bible teaches that God created woman from the side of the man—not from his head to rule over him, not from his feet to be trampled under by him, but from his side, near his heart, to be protected and loved by him. In that awareness, I ask you to repeat after me: I _____ (groom), take you, _____ (bride), to be my wife; to care for, to encourage, to lead, and to love from this day forward until death do us part.

_____ (bride), the Bible says that God brought the woman to the man to cooperate with him, to share with him, and to respond to him. In that awareness I ask you to repeat after me: I, _____ (bride), take you, _____ (groom), to be my husband; to care for, to encourage, to obey, and to love from this day forward until death do us part.

Exchange of Rings

Giving and receiving of the rings is rich with spiritual lessons for marriage. They speak of acceptance, trust, purity, and love. The beauty of their material and the uniqueness of their form point to the ideal marital state.

Do you, _____ (groom), give this ring to _____ (bride) as a token of your love for her?

Response: I do.

Will you, _____ (bride), take this ring as a token of _____ (groom's) love for you and will you wear it as a token of your love for him?

Response: I will.

Now join your right hands.

Pronouncement

The rings have been exchanged. You have repeated your vows to each other. Now, with the blessings of your friends and families and with the sweet smile of the Lord Jesus upon you, I pronounce you husband and wife. "What therefore God hath joined together, let not man put asunder" (Mark 10:9).

Benediction

Our Heavenly Father, as we bow in this place where Your presence is so very real to us, we thank You for all the blessings You have brought into our lives personally. We thank You for the difference that Jesus makes. We thank You for His love and for His grace that has given to us salvation, for the privilege of serving Jesus and for wonderful families. Lord, we thank You for this beautiful occasion which has brought us together. We thank You for _____ (groom) and for giving to our daughter such a fine Christian young man. We thank You for the parents who have guided him and directed him, and brought him to this place where he is such a testimony for the Lord Jesus.

I pray that You will be with him, and You will give him wisdom, that You will help him as he grows and matures, that Jesus shall become more and more real in his life. Use him as he preaches the gospel. May he be instrumental in bringing literally thousands of people to know our Savior. Then, our Father, we thank You for _____ (bride). We thank you for giving her to us. Now, Heavenly Father, as we have given her to you twenty-four years ago, we give her to _____ (groom) today. Bless her and use her and make her a blessing to him. For we make our prayer in Jesus' Name. Amen.

Presentation

It is my happy privilege to introduce to you Mr. and Mrs. _____ (groom's full name).

Recessional

Jerry Vines (Father of Joy, the bride)
Co-pastor, First Baptist Church
Jacksonville, Florida

Gene Williams (Father of Tim, the groom)
President, Luther Rice Theological Seminary
Jacksonville, Florida

Ceremony 23

Processional

Introduction

Because of God's leadership, we have come to this wonderful time of commitment and celebration. I believe we are standing in a place hallowed by the actual presence of God and illumined by the smile of His approval. Just as Jesus honored the wedding at Cana with His precious presence, so we believe that He is both Guest and Host at this wedding. Once again He will perform a miracle as He turns the water of singleness into the wine of oneness. I would like to ask the parents to come forward at this time. (The parents' vows are optional.)

Parents' Vows

Mr. and Mrs. _____ (groom's parents) and Mr. and Mrs. _____ (bride's parents), your presence at this time is a rich testimony of the importance of family ties.

You have encouraged _____ (groom) and
_____ (bride) to come to this moment of
oneness. You are giving your children to one of
life's greatest adventures.

You have raised your children to let them go
their own way. In their going they shall come
again to share their maturity, their joys, and
their sorrows with you. They confirm for you
that you have fulfilled your task in the Lord.

Therefore, I also ask you mothers and fathers
to make a vow, just as these two will do.

Do you, _____ (groom's father), and
_____ (groom's mother), support
_____ (groom) and _____ (bride) in
their choice of each other, and will you encourage them to build a home marked by openness,
understanding, mutual sharing, and spiritual
growth? Do you?

Response: We do.

Do you _____ (bride's father), and
_____ (bride's mother), support
_____ (groom) and _____ (bride) in
their choice of each other, and will you encourage them to build a home marked by openness,
understanding, mutual sharing, and spiritual
growth?

Response: We do.

Mr. and Mrs. _____ (groom's parents) and Mr. and Mrs. _____ (bride's

parents), thank you for your instruction, protection, and provision that have helped to bring this couple to this time.

Prayer

Biblical Message to Couple and Congregation

I. God's Word gives us the original ideal for marriage.

In Genesis we read:

"And Adam gave names to all cattle, and to the fowl of the air, and to every beast of the field; but for Adam there was not found an help meet for him. And the Lord God caused a deep sleep to fall upon Adam, and he slept; and he took one of his ribs, and closed up the flesh instead thereof; And the rib, which the Lord God had taken from man, made he a woman, and brought her unto the man. And Adam said, This is now bone of my bones, and flesh of my flesh: she shall be called Woman, because she was taken out of man. Therefore shall a man leave his father and his mother, and shall cleave unto his wife; and they shall be one flesh. And they were both naked, the man and his wife, and were not ashamed" (Gen. 2:20-25).

In order for you, _____ (groom), and you, _____ (bride), to have a marriage that is a duet and not a duel, you must understand God's blueprint for marriage. Moses not only wrote of God's original plan for marriage, but Jesus also referred to this passage in Matthew 19, as did Paul in Ephesians 5.

A. Christian marriage was desired by God for His people.

It was created *for the purpose of human pleasure.* We see the phrase over and over again, "God saw that it was good," in the description of His creation. This is the first time in all the Bible that God says something is not good. It was not good for man to be alone. In the original Hebrew, it is an emphatic negative that appears first in the phrase. Literally, it states, "Not good is man's aloneness." Unless God has called a person to a life of celibacy and singleness, it is not good to be alone. The Lord desires that we know the wonderful pleasure of marriage.

Marriage was also desired by God *for the purpose of human partnership.* God created woman to be a "helpmeet" or a helping partner for man. The Hebrew indicates that this is someone who "assists another to reach complete fulfillment." It is also used in the Old Testament of one rescuing another. Man had a gnawing need that could only be met by woman, one "suitable for him," literally "corresponding to" him. She would provide the missing pieces to the puzzle of his existence. Augustine was right: "If God meant woman to rule over man, He would have taken her out of Adam's head. Had He designed her to be his slave, He would have taken her from his feet. But God took woman out of man's side, for He made her to be a helpmeet."

B. Christian marriage is also determined by God.

Love's preparation occurred as God caused Adam to sleep in His Will. Both of you have been waiting on God's timing and for His best. The Lord has prepared you for this moment. That often difficult time of waiting is over.

You are also learning about love's revelation. When Adam saw Eve, he exclaimed, "This is now bones of my bones and flesh of my flesh" (See Gen. 2:23). It was love at first sight. As the *Living Bible* states, "This is it!" They received each other as God's perfect and beautiful gifts. God had truly revealed His love to them in fleshly form. As James put it, "Every perfect gift is from above" (Jas. 1:17). In this wedding ceremony you are acknowledging that you will continue to receive that gift for the rest of your days. You are saying in effect: "Lord, this is exactly what I've needed. I cannot improve on your gift at all."

Adam said, "This is bone of *my* bones and flesh of *my* flesh" (author's italics). God also desires that we understand love's possessions. He is responsible for Eve. She belongs to him, not as a thing but as a treasure. "So husbands ought also to love their own wives as their own bodies" (Eph. 5:28, NASB).

This receiving and giving is particularly expressed in what the Bible calls "giving and blessing." You bless each other through the spoken word. It is certainly true that death and life are in the power of the tongue (see Prov. 18:21). The death and life of your marriage will be determined by how you speak to each other—with words of kindness and affirmation or with words of criticism and anger. Remember that Solomon praised his wife on seven different occasions in the Song of Solomon, saying, "Behold, you are fair, my love." These statements will enrich and preserve your marriage: "I love you." "I am so grateful God gave you to me." "I was wrong, will you forgive me?"

**II. We must not only consider God's
original ideal but the actual
principles for Christian marriage
that are involved in this idea.**

A. We must leave our parents.

You can cut the apron strings without severing the heart cords. We must remember that the constellation of the family includes satellite members. Though we leave, we do not abandon, ignore, or mistreat parents. We simply change relationships. But the wife's leader and lover is the husband.

B. We also need to cleave to each other.

This word means to glue or to cling. Marriage is for life. God sees it as a covenant, according to Malachi 2:14-15. To break the covenant is to violate a sacred commitment. You must enter this covenant with no thought of a back door. Marriage is seen in the New Testament as an illustration of the relationship between Christ and His church. 'Till death do us part is not a verbal formality but a spiritual reality. For many it is 'till *debt* do us part or 'till *disagreement* do us part. Decide today that you will never talk about or even think of getting a divorce. Don't use it as a weapon when you become angry. Surrender is not an option if you want to win a war or succeed in a marriage.

To cleave indicates an adhesive. Jesus Christ is the glue that will hold you together. He wants to be Lord of your emotions; this brings romance. He wants to be Lord of your mind; this brings understanding. He wants to be the Lord of your spirit; this brings servanthood and communion. Surrender to Him totally, yielding your body as a living sacrifice.

C. The third principle is that we are to weave together.

We become one flesh. God's beautiful pattern is that one plus one equals one. Unity is not uniformity; Eve was not a female Adam. It is the acceptance of each other's uniqueness. It is the blending of two tributaries into one channel that flows in the same direction.

D. We must not only weave together but achieve intimacy.

Again, this is seen in the one-flesh relationship. When all of the other factors come together, then physical union is truly complete and beautiful. The Bible says that the man and his wife were both naked and were not ashamed (See Gen. 2:25). They had a beautiful relationship that was free from guilt. But this aspect of the relationship comes last, not first. The Hebrew term "naked" suggest the idea of laid bare, emphasizing total and complete nakedness. There were no hidden agendas or fears. There was total transparency. Intimacy is not the answer to a shaky marriage but the result of a solid marriage.

Adam and Eve realized their nakedness and felt guilty when they sinned. God's answer to sin was the death of an animal whose skins would cover the first couple. It was then prophesied that one would come and die for the sins of the world. His name is Jesus Christ. He gave His blood that our sins might be forgiven. Jesus Christ is the answer to loneliness, guilt, and fear. It is our prayer that all who hear this ceremony will come to Him in repentance and faith.

The Couple's Vows

I now want to ask you both a very important question. _____ (groom), do you totally commit yourself to this woman to be all that God and all that she needs you to be?

Response: I do.

And do you, _____ (bride), totally commit yourself to _____ (groom) to be all that God and he needs you to be?

Response: I do.

Now, I would have you seal your vows with the rings. The ring has been used to seal significant covenants. The circle is an emblem of eternity, showing your lasting devotion to each other. The precious substance indicates how lasting and imperishable is the love that you pledge to each other. You place it on each other's

fingers publicly as an indication of your full
commitment before these witnesses. Its perfect
symmetry and unbroken form represent the
unity that God seeks to bring into your life. It
signifies the joining of two lives to form one perfect union. Now, _____ (groom), please
place this ring on your beloved's finger and repeat after me phrase by phrase: I, _____
(groom), take you, _____ (bride), as my
lawfully and spiritually wedded wife / I promise
to forsake all others / and cleave only to you / I
promise to love/honor/comfort / and spiritually
edify you / I take you from this day forth / for
better or for worse / in riches and in poverty / in
sickness and in health / till death do us part / I
promise to pray for you / to live with you in an
understanding way / to grant you honor / as a
fellow heir of the grace of life / and to forgive
you / as God has forgiven me / I promise to give
myself to you / as Christ gave Himself for us / to
fulfill my duty to you / and to be your spiritual
leader / Therefore, I receive you / as God's
lovely gift to me.

Now, _____ (bride), would you please
place the ring on his finger and repeat after
me? . . . I, _____ (bride), take you,
_____ (groom) as my lawfully and spiritually wedded husband / I promise to forsake all
others / and cleave only to you / I promise to
love/honor /comfort / and spiritually edify you /

I take you from this day forth / for better or for worse / in riches and in poverty / in sickness and in health / till death do us part / I promise to pray for you / to seek to understand you / to forgive you as God has forgiven me / and to be in loving subjection to you as God's man in our home / I promise to adorn myself / as a holy woman with a meek and quiet spirit / I want to be an excellent wife / whose worth is far above jewels / Therefore, I receive you / as God's beautiful gift to me.

Pronouncement

You have both pledged your love to each other before these witnesses. Therefore, by the authority granted to me by the living God through His church and in accordance with the laws of this state, I joyfully pronounce you husband and wife. As someone said, "When you share a joy, it is doubled, and when you share a sorrow, it is halved." We pledge to you our prayers and continued concern. We love you. _____ (groom), you may now kiss your bride. I present to you Mr. and Mrs. _____ (groom's full name).

Recessional

Hayes Wicker, Pastor
First Baptist Church
Lubbock, Texas

Ceremony 24

Processional

Introduction

Dearly beloved, we are gathered here in the sight of God and in the presence of these witnesses to join together _____ (bride) and _____ (groom) by the wonderful ties of marriage. God Himself is the One who has ordained marriage on the basis of family life and the hope for honorable human society.

Since they have become Christians, _____ (bride) and _____ (groom) have come to understand that Christian marriage is to be a permanent relationship between a man and a woman freely and fully committed to each other as companions for life.

We must understand that, first, *Christian marriage is a covenant of faith*. The old life had faith only in self; the new life has faith in Jesus Christ. It requires of both man and woman openness of life and thought, freedom from doubt and suspicion, and commitment to speak the truth in love as they grow up in Christ who is the head of the church. This faith is the very foundation of their relating to each other on a daily basis.

Second, even in the conscious remembrance of past failures that could destroy all sense of hope and forgiveness, *Christian marriage is a covenant of hope that endures all things,* in which both husband and wife commit themselves to interpret each other's behavior with understanding and compassion, never giving up trying to communicate with each other.

The third description of marriage is: *it is a covenant of love in which both husband and wife empty themselves of their own concerns* and take upon themselves the concerns of each other in loving each other as Christ loved the church and gave Himself for her.

_____ (groom), you and _____ (bride) have come to realize no one really understands what love is. Marriage outside of Jesus Christ is only a human struggle with two people sharing only two-thirds of their lives—the body and the soul. Without Christ, they cannot share their spiritual lives. Marriage is deeper than any agreement between a man and a woman. It should involve man, woman, and Almighty God. It is a three-way relationship.

The Bible teaches: Love is patient, love is kind, and envies no one. Love is never boastful nor conceited. It is never rude, never selfish, not quick to take offense. Love keeps no score of wrongs, love does not gloat over the other person's sins, but delights in the truth. There is no limit to its faith, its hope and its endurance. Love never comes to an end. In a word, there are three things that last forever—faith, hope and love. But the greatest of these is love (1 Cor. 13:4-8a,13).

_____ (Groom) and _____ (bride), I am glad you understand that this covenant of marriage is not to be entered into superficially or lightly, but rather soberly and in full reverence to God. Thus, marriage is the binding of two hearts, two purposes, two souls, two lifestyles into one heart, one purpose, one lifestyle, protected by God and carried forth by the bonds of permanent endowment.

Now, who gives this woman to be married to this man?

Response: Her mother and I.

Prayer

Dear Father in heaven, when we think of Your love and grace that would bring Jesus from heaven's glory to earth's agony, we must kneel in awe, reverence, and worship. Lord, we want to declare our love for You at this moment. We praise You, Father, that there is therefore no condemnation to those who are in Christ Jesus, and we thank You that those who by faith have entered your family as "born-again" children are no longer strangers or aliens, but fellow citizens with the saints already seated in heavenly places in Christ Jesus.

How we praise You for our inheritance in Christ through His shed blood on Calvary as He paid the penalty for our sin. And we pray even today for men and women and young people who may not know Christ as personal Savior, that they would, by faith, receive Him as the God of their lives. For it is in Jesus' name that we pray. Amen.

Vows

You, _____ (groom) and _____ (bride), having come to me signifying your desire to be formally united in marriage, and being assured you are scripturally qualified with several months of preparation and counseling, and that no legal, moral, or spiritual barriers hinder this proper union, I ask you to join your right hands and respond to these questions:

_____ (groom), in taking the woman whom you hold by the right hand to be your wife, you must promise to live together with her in a cove-

nant of faith, of hope and love, according to the
intention of God for your lives through Jesus
Christ. You must promise to listen to her innermost thoughts, and to be considerate and helpful in your support of her. You must promise to
protect her and stand by her through all the
hard times as well as the good, never withholding your love from her, but giving it freely,
gladly, and without reservation. You must
promise to love her above all others and to accept full responsibility for her every necessity
until death alone shall part you. Do you so
promise?

Response: I do.

_____ (bride), in taking the man who
holds you by the right hand to be your husband,
you must promise to live together with him in
the covenant of faith, of hope and love, according to the intention of God for your lives
through Jesus Christ. You must promise to listen to his innermost thoughts, to be considerate
and helpful in your support of him. You must
promise to accept his protection, and to stand
by him through all the hard times as well as the
good, never withholding your love from him,
but giving it freely, gladly, and without reservation. You must promise to love him above all
others and to accept full responsibility for his

every necessity until death alone shall part you. Do you so promise?

Response: I do.

_____ (groom), will you repeat now after me your solemn vow?

Groom: I, _____ (groom), take you, _____ (bride), to be my wedded wife, to strengthen and to encourage, from this day forward, for better or worse, in sickness and in health, to love and to cherish 'til death do us part.

_____ (bride), will you repeat after me now your solemn vow?

Bride: I, _____ (bride), take you _____ (groom), to be my wedded husband, to strengthen and to encourage, from this day forward, for better or worse, in sickness and in health, to love and to cherish, 'til death do us part.

Rings

_____ (groom), do you have anything of value that you wish to give _____ (bride) as an expression of your love for her? May I see it? (Takes ring from best man.)

From the beginning of time a small band of metal has been given to demonstrate the joining of people in relationships; and through the ages, this circlet, most prized of all jewels, has come to its greatest honor, symbolically seen at the marriage altar. This beautiful material, worn in love and commitment, becomes the symbol of the true and abiding character of a God-formed marriage. (Instruct the groom to place ring on third finger of bride's left hand and hold in place while groom repeats after the minister.)

_____ (bride), with this ring I give my love, and everything I have I share with you, in the Name of the Father, the Son, and the Holy Spirit.

_____ (bride), will you receive this ring as a token of _____ (groom's) love for you, and will you wear it as a token of your love for him?

Response: I will.

_____ (bride), do you have something of value which you wish to give _____ (groom) as an expression of your love for him? May I see it? (Takes ring from maid/matron of honor. Instructs bride to place the ring on the third finger of groom's left hand and repeat after the minister.)

_____ (Groom), with this ring, I give you my love, and everything I have I share with you, in the Name of the Father, the Son, and the Holy Spirit.

_____ (groom), will you receive this ring as a token of _____ (bride's) love for you, and will you wear it as a token of your love for her?

Response: I will. (Couple will kneel when prayer bench is utilized.)

Prayer

Now, through the touching words written by Saint Francis of Assisi, let us pray: "Eternal God, make us instruments of Thy peace. Where hate rules, let us bring love; where malice, forgiveness; where disputes, reconciliation; where error, truth; where doubt, belief; where sorrow, joy. O Lord, let us strive more to comfort others than to be comforted; to understand others more than to be understood; to love others more than to be loved. For he who gives, receives; he who forgets himself, finds; and he who forgives, receives forgiveness; and dying, we rise again to eternal life, through Jesus Christ our Lord."

Pronouncement

_____ (groom) and _____ (bride), now having pledged your faith in and love to each other, and having expressed your commitment before God, and in the fellowship of this Christian community, and having given yourselves completely to each other, declaring it publicly by the giving and receiving of rings; now, acting in the authority given to me by the laws of this state, and looking to God for His continued approval, I pronounce you husband and wife in the name of the Father, and the Son, and the Holy Spirit. Let us pray.

Prayer

Dear Heavenly Father, how I thank you for the strong desire on the part of _____ (groom) and _____ (bride) to build a truly Christian marriage. I pray that their love, demonstrated by unselfishness, faithfulness, trust and respect for each other, might be a wonderful testimony to those around them. Father, Your Word now is sanctifying, or setting apart, this act of marriage. Help all of us to know that _____ (groom) and _____ (bride) will become one flesh, supernaturally, by the Spirit of the living God. And we pray Your supernatural blessings on this new home and any children who arrive. Fill them now with your Holy Spirit. In Jesus' name we pray. Amen.

You may kiss the bride.

Now, I present to you Mr. and Mrs. _____ (groom's full name).

Recessional

> Jim Wilson
> Evangelist
> Orlando, Florida

Ceremony 25

Processional

Welcome

On behalf of the bride and groom, it is my privilege to say a personal word of greeting and welcome. You are special in their hearts and in their lives, and they are honored that you have made the effort to be here and to share in this tremendous time of covenant-making.

I think it is important that we remember that these two young people met in the church, which is the best place to meet your mate. And in spite of—and in some cases because of—everything all of us could do, they fell in love. It has been thrilling for us to see from a close vantage point the integrity, the gentleness, and the manner in which they have conducted themselves during these weeks and months of courtship.

Prayer

Father, we thank You for _____ (bride) and _____ (groom). We thank You for the sincerity which we see in their lives, for the love which they have for You, for their sense of call into Thy kingdom, and for the way in which they have put Thee, O Lord, first in all things. Dear Father, we trust that as they grow together, the experience of these moments will always be sacred. We pray that in this hour a home might be established upon which You will bestow all good things. May this marriage and this home be a testimony and an example to others of what it means to be sold out to You. May their primary purpose in life always be to do Your will. We are thankful that, in Your sovereignty, You have brought together these two who have so much to give and so many years, we trust, left to serve Your kingdom. Lord, we lean upon You in this hour, and pray through Jesus Christ our Lord. Amen.

Introduction

I think it is interesting to observe and fascinating to remember that the first contract in a human sense was established by God Himself when He uttered the nuptial vows there in the Garden of Eden. With Adam and Eve, He established the home and marriage as the institution that would be the foundation of honorable, noble, and godly living.

We know also that Jesus selected a marriage feast for the background of His first miracle. According to Hebrew tradition, this was not so much a formal affair as it was a time of celebration. It was a time of prayer and a time of feasting, a time of laughter, and a time of reverence. It was a time of ritual in which the whole community would participate. In this way the townspeople would acknowledge that they had been a part of the engagement process, that they were a part of the marriage ceremony, and that they would be a continuing part of the couple's life together.

At such a traditional celebration Jesus performed the first miracle of His earthly ministry. He selected a marriage ceremony as the setting for bringing the supernatural into the natural domain.

Paul, the militant missionary apostle, selected marriage as a symbol of that relationship between Jesus Christ and the church. Paul said that the husband is to love his wife as Christ loved the church and gave His life for her. That is strong love. It is divine, *agape love*.

And then Paul addresses the wife's role. She is to be faithful to her husband in all things. In fact, to this life-giving love the husband gives to the wife, the wife is to respond with an attitude of reverence toward her husband. How easy it is to reverence someone who is willing to give his life for you on a daily basis.

Paul says it is essential that the husband and wife forsake all others. Except for their relationship to the Lord, that wife and husband are to have no higher priority than each other. Even a vocational call is to take a secondary place to that call to love and to respond to the needs and concerns of your mate. Even a call to parenthood is subordinate to the marriage relationship. Thus, these two, husband and wife, forsaking all others, become one in thought, in intent, in hope, and in all the concerns of this present life.

Who gives this woman to be married to this man? (Father, family member, or friend responds with, "I do," "We do," "Her mother and I," etc.).

You, _____ (bride), and you, _____ (groom), having come to me signifying your desire to be united in marriage, have assured me that no legal, moral, or religious barriers hinder this proper union. I now ask you to join right hands and to heed the following words.

Vows

_____ (groom), if you will, say these words after me? I, _____ (groom), take thee, _____ (bride), to be my wedded wife; to have and to hold, from this day forward, for better, for worse, for richer, for poorer, in sickness and in health; to love and to cherish, 'till death do us part, according to God's holy ordinance. And thereto, I plight thee my troth.

_____ (bride), if you will, say these words after me? I, _____ (bride), take thee, _____ (groom), to be my wedded husband; to have and to hold, from this day forward, for better, for worse, for richer, for poorer, in sickness and in health; to love and to cherish, till death do us part, according to God's holy ordinance. And thereto, I give thee my troth.

Do you, _____ (groom), give this ring to _____ (bride), as a token of your love for her?

Response: I do.

_____ (bride), will you receive this ring and wear it as a symbol of _____ (groom's) love for you?

Response: I will.

_____ (bride), do you give this ring to _____ (groom) as a token of your love for him?

Response: I do.

_____ (Groom), will you receive this ring and wear it as a symbol of _____ (bride's) love for you?

Response: I will.

Years ago in a little village, the city council was meeting in an effort to cut expenses when they noticed a relatively small amount allocated to the "Keeper of the Springs." A frugal man asked, "Why are we paying this fee? What does the Keeper of the Springs do?"

Another member of the council said, "I'm not sure, but I think there's an old mountain man who stays up in the mountains and cleans out all the springs and all the little creeks up there which flow into the river that fills the reservoir and provides our drinking water."

They all agreed, "That's a ridiculous fee to pay somebody we never see. We don't even know if he does his job, so let's just cut that out of the budget." They voted unanimously no longer to employ the strange mountain man who supposedly kept all the springs clean at the headwaters before they flowed into the river that provided water for the people to drink.

During the first year, people began to notice that the water wasn't quite as sparkling as before, but "sparkle" wasn't all that important. During the second year, the people noticed that the water had changed color, and some even mentioned that there had been more sickness that year than in past years. During the third year, the pollution in the water was readily visible. Even with the purification process, the water in their reservoir simply was not clean. That same year, an epidemic broke out in the village that cost many people their lives. Authorities and chemists were brought in to test the drinking water, and they discovered contamination. When they traced the contamination back to its source, they discovered, at huge expense, that the waters there in the mountain had become polluted because no one had been routinely cleaning out the springs.

The city council met again and agreed, "Let's go find the old keeper of the springs and re-employ him because we can't live in this village without him."

_____ (groom), and _____ (bride), you are going to be busy during your days together. A lot of people are going to be asking and pushing and shoving and making demands. You can spend a day without getting into the Scriptures and without prayer, and nobody will notice. You could probably spend a week, and very few would notice any difference. You might become a little edgy, and things might not run quite as smoothly. You might even go a month, or several months, without really spending time with God. And even those who know you best might not observe any difference, except in the little things.

But how important it is in your individual relationships with the Lord, and in your relationship as a couple with Him, that you make sure the springs of life are clean and clear on a daily, and even hourly, basis as you seek God's best in your home.

Now, I share a verse, one that absolutely works when it is applied. _____ (bride), you apply it to _____ (groom). _____ (groom), you apply it to _____ (bride), and on the authority of God's Word, your marriage will be beautiful, and it will be blessed.

"Be ye kind one to another, tenderhearted, forgiving one another, even as God for Christ's sake hath forgiven you" (Eph. 4:32).

Pronouncement

Acting by the authority vested in me by the laws of the state of _____ and looking to heaven for divine sanction, I now pronounce you husband and wife in the presence of God and these assembled witnesses. Let no man put asunder what God Himself hath joined together. Let us pray.

Prayer

Our Heavenly Father, we are grateful to Thee for the Christian homes which have nurtured these two people, and for the fact that they have fallen in love with each other. Dear Father, we trust that Your hand will be upon their lives as they live together as one, just as Your hand of maturity and blessing has been upon them before they knew each other. Father, guide them during stormy times and come close to them, especially during times of great blessing. Give to this couple, we pray, steadiness, consistency, and faithfulness to Thee, so their relationship will always be clean and holy before Thee. For this is our prayer as family and friends, made in the name of Him who is the foundation of every house that is a home, and who keeps the springs of our lives clear and clean. We pray in Jesus' name. Amen.

Introduction

It is my privilege to present to you Mr. and Mrs. _____ (groom's full name).

Recessional

H. Edwin Young, Pastor
Second Baptist Church
Houston, Texas